Graduation Day

ALANA MCINTYRE

Copyright © 2011 Alana McIntyre

1,000 Pages Publishing

All rights reserved. No part of this book may be reproduced, scanned, or distributed in any printed or electronic form without permission.

ISBN-13: **978-0-9838003-0-9**
ISBN: 0983800308

Graduation Day is a work of fiction. Names, characters, places, and incidents either are the product of the author's imagination or are used fictitiously, and any resemblance to actual persons, living or dead, businesses, companies, events, or locales is entirely coincidental.

To my family…

Thank you for your unconditional love, support, and encouragement.
You've made my dreams come true.

To God be the glory…

CONTENTS

1	Ellie at Birth	1
2	The Way In	5
3	Ellie at Five	21
4	The Welcome	27
5	Ellie at Ten	40
6	The Waiting and Watching	45
7	Ellie at Fifteen	59
8	The Walk	65
9	Ellie at Twenty	82
10	The Whys	88
11	Ellie at Twenty-Five	101
12	The Way It Will Be	109
13	Ellie at Thirty	124
14	The Waves	132
15	Ellie at Thirty-Five	149

1 / ELLIE AT BIRTH

Ellie Mathews was almost complete. Dark hair like her mother, green eyes with a sprinkle of gold like her father. Left-handed like her grandfather, the skill to draw like two of her uncles, and a sensitivity and awareness that were unique only to her. The mixture was coming together exactly as prescribed. A new creation, a perfect combination of familiarity and individuality.

Soon, this spark of life with all the right ingredients would be released to earth, and then she would have a chance to learn and to grow and to take all that she had been given and make it her own.

***

When Juliet Mathews began to feel a little nauseous in the mornings and the aroma of her favorite enchilada dinner made her groan in agony, she knew something was up. She called her doctor and made an appointment without telling Mark. If the news was good, she wanted to surprise him. If it was bad, she didn't even want to bother him. The pressure at work lately had been intense, and she did not want to add to that stress in any way.

This would be just the thing to cheer Mark up. Raised in a tight knit brood of four brothers, Mark loved the idea of having a big family. When their first daughter had been born, he slid easily into his role as father and couldn't wait to have more. It had only taken them a few months to conceive Grace, but a second child hadn't come that easily. Though Mark had never expressed his disappointment, Juliet knew he was just waiting for her to surprise him. And she was just as anxious to provide that source of joy for him. It was disappointing to realize month after month that she had failed.

Later that afternoon, Juliet tied the bow around the waist of her favorite dress a little looser as she completed the finishing touches on dinner. The report from the doctor had been a good one, and Juliet sent her three-year-old Grace to stay with a neighbor for the night. She watched for Mark's car to drive up, and she pulled him inside as soon as he got to their front door. She smothered his questions with sweet kisses and held up the doctor's report with tears in her eyes.

As he took her softly in his arms and gently rubbed her barely-expanding tummy, Juliet let out a sigh of relief. How had she gotten the life of her dreams? A husband who loved her, not one but two children to lead through life and cheer on through whatever it might bring -- a future and a hope. She felt like the luckiest woman in the world. This life would be nothing like the one she had left behind several hundred miles away. Nothing like the disappointment and abandonment she had felt. She would never, ever do that to her family.

***

Ellie's time had finally come, and an anxious excitement fluttered within her. Somewhere in the distance, she could hear loud voices and a deep moaning. Some of the voices were familiar and though they seemed to be in distress, she felt calmed by them. Soon, she noticed an acceleration deep within her and felt herself being pulled closer and closer to a light. This was the moment her young spirit had yearned for over the past nine months.

Suddenly, everything was happening very quickly. Ellie tried to push back against the intense pull she was feeling, but there was no stopping the momentum. A terror of the unknown filled her innocence and, as the light overwhelmed her, she cried out. She cried and cried until a comforting voice and familiar scent held her close, until she could no longer remember the reason for her tears.

***

Mark wiped the dark hair from Juliet's forehead and kissed her softly. He beamed with pride as he held his eldest daughter's hand and let his new baby girl grab hold of his finger.

"What should we name her?" he asked, surprised as he realized they had never actually agreed on such an important decision.

Juliet thought for a moment and then replied with a sureness in her voice.

"Eleanor," she said. "After your aunt. She never had any daughters but always treated me like one. Let's do that for her."

Mark nodded, touched by his wife's thoughtfulness, even in her exhaustion. They had never even discussed that, but somehow it seemed perfect.

"My little Ellie," he said and gently rubbed the dark fluff on top of her head.

As Juliet watched him, she exhaled deeply and tried to fully embrace the moment. Here it was, her perfect dream come true: a happy and healthy family…an endless future stretching before them with nowhere to go but up. As she closed her eyes and drifted to sleep, she was thankful once again that the man she married was nothing like her father and that her daughters would never know the brokenness of her past. She would protect them from that at all costs.

***

Kind eyes watched the scene unfolding down below. Avia was so happy for this young family. She had been sent to watch over Juliet since Juliet herself was born; she had seen the difficult times that Juliet had been through and was thrilled to see her joy. And now, as she spread her wings and took flight in a flash of unseen light, Avia wished she could whisper to her charge: *"Hold them close, dear. Enjoy this time, and make the most of every moment. Graduation Day will be here soon."*

2 / THE WAY IN

Graduate #1

The man was old, tired, and alone in his hospital room. Doctors and nurses flowed through the doors like tributaries in and out of the sea. But he didn't notice them anymore. They had stopped providing any relief for him months ago. The last stage of colon cancer was gruesome and painful, and as much as he wanted to stay alive for his children and even more, his grandchildren, the fight had left him. His aches were bone deep, and the morphine could only coat his agony. When he moved, it hurt. When he sat still, it hurt. The pain never quite went away. This evening, his breathing had become more labored. His body and all his functions seemed to be slowing down. He was both anxious and excited that the end might be near.

His eldest daughter, an overworked lawyer whose praise he would sing to anyone who would listen, was supposed to be coming by that evening to check on him. His three children had set up a rotation and they were faithful to it, though their visits had started to become shorter and shorter, and he recently noticed more and more glances toward the door as soon as they arrived. His fourth child would never come for a visit; in fact, he would never get to meet him at all. But that was how it had been arranged, and he had no desire to change that now. He only worried about what they would think of him after he was gone, when they all found out.

He knew it was no fun visiting an old man. The hospital reeked of death and dying. Even visitors who walked the halls couldn't help but be sucked into the depressingly hopeless state of his floor. It was beginning to overwhelm him, and he was tired of being a drain on his family.

He didn't like for his grandchildren to see him like this – weak and frail and incapable. He wanted them to think of him as a big bear of a man, throwing them into the air and chasing them until they laughed so hard no sound would come out. Those were the memories he thought of most now, and the realization that those days were behind him made continuing to live seem pointless and the end seem more bearable.

He was waiting for his daughter to arrive, and he wished she would hurry. He had words to say that she needed to hear – how proud he was, how much she reminded him of her mother, how she would need to watch out for the rest of them, how sorry he was for the mistakes he had made but that he had always loved them.

He had thoughts of legacy, both spiritually and physically. Did he have anything of worth that he was leaving behind? Had he taught his children enough; had he prepared them for a world without him? Had he taught them about forgiveness and tolerance? He knew his children would need both when they found out the truth.

He could feel the strength seeping out of his bones, and he glanced at the clock. His usually punctual daughter was late, and he worried that there wouldn't be enough time. He grabbed the pen and paper near his bed, ready to scrawl out his last wishes, thoughts, and an impromptu addition to his will.

A little while later, his daughter entered the room. She had an excuse ready for the old man, and his favorite pasta (though forbidden at the hospital) was hidden in her purse. Her father was sleeping quietly, and she sat down softly in the chair by his bed. She pulled out her phone and waited for a few moments. He usually stirred quickly, and she didn't want to disturb him.

Twenty minutes had passed when the alarms started ringing. They were shrill, monotone beeps that caused the nurses and doctors to flood the room. The daughter jumped to her feet, at once terrified and in shock.

They excused her from the room but she stared through the windows and watched as futile attempts were made to revive the man who had always been her biggest supporter. After what did not seem like a long enough time at all, they came out and the young doctor frowned and relayed the news that she already knew. He then quietly left her alone with her father's body.

She cried softly as she touched his hand, confused at her feelings of sadness and relief. She was happy he was no longer in pain and embarrassingly thankful she would no longer have to fight her already crammed schedule to find time to visit him. As she turned to leave, she nudged something with the edge of her well-worn pumps. At her feet, she found a notepad and picked it up. Written in his thin, scratchy handwriting were three words: *Love...forgiveness...hope.*

Then, further down the page, he continued: *With these three things, you have it all. Without them, nothing else matters.*

She wiped the tears from her eyes and wondered at her father's words. He wasn't usually a sentimental man; she knew that he loved them all, but she couldn't think of the last time he had actually said it. It was strange for her now, to think of him as a vulnerable, fragile being. As they all were. She squeezed his hand tightly once more and sighed deeply when he didn't squeeze back. Then, she wiped the tears away for a final time that night and stuffed the notepad in her purse. She had a funeral to plan.

***

Graduate #2

The air was hot, dry, and it seemed to steal the life from all who tried to breathe it. The ground was hard and painful to bare feet, especially those that had walked for miles in the unrelenting sun to arrive at their destination.

The family sat around a small drinking hole, surrounded in part by an antelope, a mother giraffe and her baby, and a few elephants. There were also some hyenas in the distance, but the family never made eye contact with them. Their yellow piercing stares invited death as they paced around the edge of the hole, waiting to take advantage of any tragedies.

Today was finally the family's turn at the hole, and they wanted to savor every moment of it. This opportunity only came once in a while, and they had to gather enough sustenance for the next several days, as well as bathe and clean the dust and dirt from their tired bodies. The family of six would first gather the water from the hole in the worn and cracking urns they had brought. Once they had secured their supply, they would spread out and bathe, taking turns so that someone was always watching the water for approaching danger.

This process could take hours, and it was usually a joyous occasion with the youngest two or three dancing about and splashing in the water and everyone drinking in as much as they possibly could handle, re-energizing their fragile bodies.

On this day however, no one was smiling, and all eyes stayed focused on the ground. They didn't want to face what today meant, that it was the last hope.

The mother held the youngest in her arms and he lay limp, draped there across her, rarely struggling or crying out. The cries were so soft, not the strong, unending wails of months before. You could barely hear his meager voice, but the mother clung to the tiny sound. The others watched and held back, though everything within them wanted to run and lap up the water and enjoy what should have been their time of relief and rejoicing.

The mother quickly brought the baby to the edge of the banks and scooped up the brown liquid for him to drink. Silently, she pleaded toward the heavens that this would be the healing medicine that would restore his life and take away the sickness.

The baby hung listless in her arms, not even managing the pitiful cry of moments ago. In fact, no sounds came out of him now. His delicate skin pulled taut against his bones, which poked through at every angle. The mother shook him softly, repeatedly cupping the water and offering it again and again.

The baby's eyes closed, and he did not even try to swallow as she continued to bring the water to his lips. The mom tried over and over, unable to relinquish this last act and give in to what it would mean if he would not drink. She could not bear to lose another.

Minutes passed slowly until they could no longer watch the desperate scene. The father came and took the baby away as the mother went to her knees, her shoulders shaking violently with large but silent sobs. The other children approached but she could not turn her attention to them. They touched her hair, lightly rubbing her back as she shook. She allowed herself a few minutes of grief, and then silently stood and turned to help her other children drink.

They watched her with sad eyes and with fear. They didn't want to drink, but she ushered the water to their quivering lips. They did not want to look at their father, but one finally took a brief glance at the silent figure.

The father sat under a nearby tree, still holding the infant tightly in his arms. The baby was not moving at all anymore and his beautiful chocolate brown eyes had opened, staring straight up into the sky without wavering.

Quickly, the oldest child pointed and called out, and they all turned to look. The father did not return their stare, but they could see his shoulders slightly shaking as well. And they all knew.

Across the flat lands, a bird called out shrilly as it chased its prey, and it echoed across the distant dunes. Then, all was still as a mother's deep wails began to rise up across the land.

***
Graduate #3

The weather forecaster had called for severe thunderstorms that night, but he hadn't paid much attention. Their town had received record-breaking rain over the past month, and it had been such a blessing to his land. Last season, the rain had not come, and the crops had not grown. He had struggled to feed his family, and it hurt him to see their hungry eyes and hear their growling stomachs.

But they had persevered, mostly through the creativity and resourcefulness of his wife. He was reminded of why he married her fourteen years ago when she managed to create a filling and fun dinner out of potatoes and macaroni and cheese. She had found ways to bring them through all year long. Now that the rain was coming down and there was relief from the heat and the hunger, he was happy and relieved, mostly for her.

And the kids. Fathering four young boys wasn't something he wished on anyone. He was so thankful for them, but he felt a tremendous responsibility to live every day as a perfect example so that they would grow up and be the kind of man he hoped to be. And not the kind of man his father had been.

Stubborn, angry, and drunk were the only memories he had of his old man. He would come in from a long day in the fields and take out his frustrations on anyone within hitting range. They all learned at a young age to stay out of reach and out of sight as much as possible.

But that wasn't the way to raise children, and he vowed never to be anything like his father. Though he knew some people who cursed their parents' mistakes only to see them reborn in their own lives, he made sure his life was the complete opposite of his father's. And he was proud of that.

The only similarity they shared was their profession. He had plowed and developed and nurtured the fifteen acres of land he inherited from his father. That had been his share of the family farm and the one good gift the old man had left him. Until lately, it had allowed him to provide for his family.

With farming, he was completely at the mercy of the weather. There was nothing he could do to make the rain come, and so now, with it all but flooding their region, he could not complain.

He had just turned his car off the loop when the first siren rang out. Deep and low and ominous, the intense sound filled the cab of his truck and made him swerve slightly off the one-lane dirt road.

He planned on ignoring it, on continuing directly into town to collect their supplies and deliver crops for sale, when he noticed the towering black cloud in front of him. The tornado had come from out of nowhere; he knew he would not have missed the massive swirling clouds, thickened by a haphazard combination of branches and random debris. Even more terrifying than the sight of the tornado was the sound. He could hear it with overpowering clearness now, even inside his truck. The deep hiss was dramatically louder than the warning siren.

For a moment, he just stopped, unsure if he should try and outrun it or get out and find a ditch. Wasn't that what the weatherman always said to do? But right then, staying put just did not seem like the right option. Quickly, he spun the truck around and started his futile attempt to outrun the monster.

Unfortunately, his little old truck was weighed down by the full trailer he was towing, and he could barely get up to 35 miles per hour. He looked up to see the tornado whirling at him at an increasing rate of speed. He punched the pedal as hard as he could with his foot, but it was to no avail.

Minutes that felt like seconds passed before the tornado caught up with him. One moment, he was driving as fast as he possibly could, and the next, he was swirling around in mid-air. It was a surreal feeling, and he kept trying to steer the wheel, to angle himself back towards the ground. But the tornado took him higher. The sound inside the beast was deafening, like a freight train plowing right through his head.

He was trying desperately to think, to figure out his best chance for survival, when the windshield shattered in front of him. Glass flew everywhere, cutting him, causing him to cry out. But before he could really feel the pain, a great force of suction ripped him from the vehicle. For a moment, he was flying and it was beautiful. Completely weightless, he could see the wide expanse of land below him and he felt amazingly free as he soared above it. Was this what heaven would be like?

The euphoric feeling would not last long. The tornado was losing power and shifting directions. An instant later, he was hurling towards the ground at a great deal of speed. If only he could hit something soft, something flexible. A large concrete building loomed in the distance. He twisted and turned and tried to direct himself as he imagined Superman might guide himself through the air. Unfortunately, he realized quickly that despite his struggling and flailing about, his line of trajectory could not be changed. He braced himself for the collision and a second later, felt nothing.

***

Graduate #4

He was four years old when the accident happened. Flashes of the fall and an ember of the pain were etched in his memory. But what he could not remember was how life had been before he'd lost the use of his legs. He could not remember what it felt like to walk.

People did not truly understand the sadness that tugged at his soul, the jealousy he felt each and every time he saw someone walk down the street or run across the path in front of him.

At 23, he was otherwise healthy and had graduated from a local college at the top of his class. But he hadn't been able to walk across the stage. He had wheeled up the ramp and down the aisle to the dean. He struggled for a minute as they handed him a diploma and reached to shake his hand. He knew everyone saw the awkward moment, and he hated their pity.

In fact, he hated that more than not being able to walk. He didn't want people to feel sorry for him; he just wanted to be capable. He wanted to be able to do what a toddler could do – put one foot in front of the other. Nothing could be more simple, or more impossible.

He didn't blame his dad for the accident, though he knew that his dad would never forgive himself. He had begged all day to go on the roof to help put up the lights. He remembered seeing all the other houses in the neighborhood lit up for Christmas, and when his dad pulled down box after box of decorations, he was desperate to help.

His mom had called out to them. She had warned them to be careful. But that's what moms do. She had softly touched his bright red hair, smoothed it out of his face, and looked him in the eye.

"Stay right by your dad, and don't let go," she said. But his dad had been the one that let go. They were almost done attaching the final strand when the boy slipped. His dad had lunged for him and caught two of his fingers. The grasp wasn't enough to hold, and the father cried out as his son fell through the air.

He would always remember that sensation of flying. An instant of freedom. And then a second later, the impact. His spinal cord had been damaged beyond repair. His parents had cried when they got the news. It would be months before he realized that the wheelchair would never leave him. He became very adept at it, but he resented it every day. He just wanted to physically do what others could do. That's all. A simple wish.

The morning after his twenty-third birthday, he took the day off from work. He rolled down to the lake across from his apartment and watched the ducks as he ate his lunch. As he finished his meal, a loud car honked in the distance. The ducks startled, and instantly three of them took to the air. He watched them as they flew. With all his heart, he wished he was one of them. What could be better than walking? Without a doubt, to soar through the sky.

He threw his trash away and rolled down the sidewalk to the bank to deposit a few of the birthday checks he received earlier that week. He waited in line patiently; he knew this was the busiest bank on this side of the city and he was in no rush. He thought of the things he might buy with his new money; perhaps something for his computer or a new video game. He loved to play the action titles; he could almost lose himself in their intensity and pretend he was the one fighting the battles.

He noticed a few people glancing his way as he wheeled through the line, and he liked to tell himself that they were admiring his fiery red hair. But he knew that wasn't the case, and it was hard not to be irritated by their curiosity.

A moment later, he realized a hush had fallen over the bank. He arched his neck to look behind him, and suddenly everything happened in slow motion. Two masked men were waving guns in the air, yelling at everyone to get down on the ground. He froze. He could not get down on the ground. Would they shoot him for disobeying? He could feel the sweat trickling down his red hair, and his heart was beating so hard he thought he could see it pounding through his shirt.

Everyone was yelling and screaming, and then one of the gunmen stopped beside him. He waited, afraid to breathe, afraid to move. The gunman was barking instructions, ignoring him completely.

At first, he was relieved for this. He was obviously not a threat. A man in a wheelchair. What could he do? But, after a minute or two, he got mad.

Why should he be ignored? He was not completely helpless. This was his chance to be a hero; he had the element of surprise on his side.

Without another thought, he thrust his body toward the enemy. For the second time in his life, he felt like he was flying.

Then, a single gunshot rang out and all was dark.

***

Graduate #5

The day that Juliet Mathews died was without significance or fanfare, as one might expect with their final moments on this earth. It was just another morning of taking the girls to school and forcing herself to attend her workout class.

The drop-off at school had been an emotionally draining one. Grace, nine, had leapt from the car with a quick goodbye and a mad dash toward her friends. There was no hesitation in her step; she was deeply engrossed with her classes, her buddies, and all that elementary school entailed. Sometimes, in the evenings, Juliet had to force her to put her schoolbooks away and join them for a walk or a quick drive to the ice cream store. She was just so content to pour all of her time and energy into this time of her life.

But Ellie, who had turned five the previous summer, had not taken to school as quickly. Each morning was filled with tears, sobs even, as she pleaded her case for staying home. She was willing to cook, clean, and even mow the lawn if necessary to keep from going to the place she dreaded the most.

When Juliet begged her to disclose the reason for her reluctance, Ellie clammed up and would not elaborate. She would simply take her mom by the hand and say she wanted to be close to her, all day long. Juliet would sigh and try to explain that it wasn't possible, but Ellie would just burst into tears again and beg for leniency.

Juliet had already been up to the school twice for talks with her teacher, and she had a feeling that another conference would be scheduled at any moment. The teachers had no explanation for it. Ellie was a bright and outgoing girl most of the time, but occasionally she would turn quiet and fade into a corner of the room. And from that moment on, there would be no participation from her.

She wasn't belligerent about it, just non-responsive; no amount of bribery or cajoling could faze her. The teachers just attributed it to a rough adjustment to kindergarten, but Juliet was worried it was something more.

Many nights, she couldn't help but cry to herself, as her husband Mark held her in his reassuring arms. What had she done wrong with Ellie? Why was she so miserable? How could she make this better? Her daughter's happiness was an utmost priority for Juliet, and she prayed each night for guidance, for solutions, for peace.

But so far, no peace had come, and Juliet was still stressing over it when she realized she was late for her workout class. In fact, it would be that realization and the small decisions that followed that would prove to be her demise.

It wasn't unusual for Juliet to be running late. This was the third time this month she knew she would miss the beginning of her class. But for some reason, today of all days, this irritated her to no end. Maybe it was because this class was one of the few things she did for herself, and she didn't want to let any of that precious "me" time slip away. Maybe it was because Mark's hours had recently been cut back at work, and she felt guilty for wasting their hard-earned money on half of a class. She had wanted to drop the class altogether, but Mark had insisted.

"All day long, you give of yourself to everyone else. This is for you. We'll save somewhere else, but you're not dropping the class."

She knew she was lucky to have such an understanding husband, but once he made up his mind about something he felt strongly about, it was difficult to get him to budge. In this case, his stubbornness worked in her favor.

She really did enjoy the class. During that hour-long adrenaline rush, she would allow herself to slip away from all the thoughts and worries of a mother, of a wife, of a woman. For those few precious moments, she would put all of her concentration into pushing herself as hard as she could and working up as much of a sweat as possible. It felt good to get that anxious energy out, and she was thankful for the release.

Afterwards, she would head home to quickly shower and change. There was never a lot of time for makeup and jewelry, but she did the basics to be presentable. She would rush to the hospital for her weekly staff meeting and to retrieve her home health assignments. Then, she would begin her tour of the town, visiting those that were too sick or too old to be at the hospital.

And so as she drove towards the haven that was her exercise class, Juliet became desperate to get there on time. She felt her speed increasing, and she was changing lanes more often than she was used to. A reckless intensity overcame her, and she could feel herself taking risks she usually wouldn't have taken.

Most days, she would stay on the side roads to go to class, enjoying the few minutes of alone time and the opportunity to think about the day ahead. Today, however, there was no serenity about her.

She contemplated the quickest way to arrive at her destination. She was pretty sure if she hopped on the highway for a few miles and took the Park Street exit, she would get there with minutes to spare.

Juliet was almost to the class when the crash happened. She'd navigated the traffic-filled highway with ease and was exiting as planned. She glanced at the clock and saw she was going to make it. As she relaxed, she realized she had forgotten to tell Mark to pick up the meat for dinner on his way home from work.

As a rule, she never used her cell phone while she was driving. It was big and bulky and she still struggled a bit to make the new contraption work. It had been an extravagant purchase, one they might have to cancel if their finances didn't turn around, but Mark had thought it was necessary since she was often in unsavory areas of town late at night.

Despite all this, Juliet convinced herself that she had to act now. She knew that if she waited until she got to class to call Mark, she would be late. And if she didn't call him now, she would forget. And then dinner would be ruined and so on; it all seemed extremely important at the time.

A combination of a familiar curve taken too fast and an ill-timed reach for her cell phone brought her up to the back of a city bus at a high rate of speed. When Juliet looked up, the rear headlights were almost in her car, and she only had an instant to think. She didn't try to swerve, but instead sighed at how stressed this would make Mark when she called him about the wrecked car. They didn't have the money for this right now.

And this was going to make her incredibly late for her class. Her dark hair flew into her face as the impact crumpled the metal body of her car. Then, all was black.

When Juliet had her flash, it was blurry and clear at the same time; bright, fuzzy lights were swirling about her and then clear snippets from her life began to play. It started early, in her childhood, with her parents. Overwhelmingly, the majority of her early memories were good ones; the bad ones seemed to fade into the background. Her fifth birthday party with the frizzy-haired doll she had asked for all year long. Her twelfth birthday when her mom finally let her get her ears pierced. The father-daughter dance where her father had given her a rose and held her hand and told her she would always be his little girl. The large weeping willow in her back yard that had provided her family with shade and the perfect cover for countless picnics and evening meals together. The old, dented, beloved truck she received for her sixteenth birthday and the freedom she felt whenever she drove it.

But not every memory was perfect, and she relived a few of the ones that had affected her the most. The fatal car wreck involving a friend during high school. The day she came home from college to find her mom crying at the kitchen table and her dad's suitcase by the front door. She saw herself holding her mom's hand later that same year at her father's funeral; her complex emotions at that point were so raw. She hated what he had done to her mother, hated how he had left them and made them feel unworthy, but he was still her father and she wanted to love him and miss him. Yet as she looked at the bleached-blonde stranger across the room from them at the funeral and remembered how she had encouraged her to call her "mommy", she wasn't sure she could ever trust another man again. Then Mark entered the scene. He looked so young and so hopeful. She tried to reach out and touch him, but the flash flew on. Mark was on his knee, proposing under the sweeping live oak where they had shared their first kiss. Mark on their wedding day, a tear in his eye that he'd quickly brushed away. Mark holding her close and promising her forever in front of all of their friends and family. When she looked into those green eyes of his, she felt like anything was possible. Their first apartment came next; she could almost smell the dirty old carpet they ripped out and felt the excitement when they discovered hardwoods underneath. Then, the pain and ecstasy of Grace's birth. She'd never felt love like that, and it filled her now. She could see Grace's chubby smile, her first steps, hear her gurgling those first words that only a parent can understand. Then Ellie entered the pictured, and again love surged inside of Juliet. And then quickly, a twinge, an ache. Ellie was smiling, growing, and then looking directly at her with tension scarred across her face. Her eyes were wide, full of tears and fear.

"Please don't leave me, Mom. I need you so much. Please..."

These desperate pleas from her precious girl caused Juliet's heart to break. She couldn't leave her family now; they had so much more life to live and she had so much more to teach them. There were so many experiences that they hadn't had yet; she wouldn't abandon them. She tried to reach out her hands toward Ellie, to pull her close. But every limb felt like it weighed a thousand pounds and despite her strongest efforts, she could not get to her. She could not move. Suddenly, the bright fuzzy light returned and the images began to fade. Juliet felt a peace and stillness overcoming her.

As soon as the paramedics arrived, they quickly surveyed the scene. Several cars were involved in the pile up, people were screaming, and several appeared to be injured. The city bus captured their attention first, and it was a few minutes before they made it to Juliet's vehicle. The assessment was fast and accurate.

"No pulse. Get the stretcher." A brief revival attempt was made, but the damage had already been done. They searched the purse that lay beside her in the seat, now splattered with blood.

Finding her ID, the paramedic muttered: "Juliet Mathews, time of death: 8:44 am."

***

The graduating class of May 14, 1988 contained 101,474 members. They came from every corner of the earth and every generation. Some had slipped in, after years of pain and discomfort; others arrived with a jolt, victims of tragic and instant demise. In the end, all had taken their last breath and entered the heavenly arena.

3 / ELLIE AT FIVE

She knew something was wrong. Ellie sat on the cafeteria bench and twirled her straight black hair, glancing repeatedly at the steady stream of cars building in the carpool line. Her mom was *always* first in line to pick her up, but today, twelve kids had already left, and Ellie still hadn't even spotted their dark gray car.

She couldn't wait to see her mom; she had to tell her about the most wonderful thing that had happened today. Ellie had been picked to read the library book to the class. Many kids in her class still couldn't read all the words in the book, but Ellie had read it out loud the whole way through. And then everyone had clapped, and she had been proud. There was actually a note from her teacher tucked inside the green take-home folder in her backpack. She couldn't wait to pull it out as soon as she hopped in the car.

But then she caught herself. She was smiling a little too much; she was feeling a little too happy inside. She looked around quickly and wondered if anyone had noticed. She wondered if it was too late.

Maybe today was the day, the day it would happen. Ellie thought this every day, but for some reason, today felt different. Ellie could feel her face getting hot, and then her eyes started to sting. She bit her lip as hard as she could; she did not want to cry again. She knew the kids would make fun of her.

For as long as she could remember, Ellie had felt a little sad. When everyone else in their family was laughing and playing and having so much fun, Ellie would catch herself. She would stop and watch the happiness around her, and she knew it was going to end. She didn't know how or when or even why, but she knew that one day, something bad was going to happen.

Often, she would try and figure out what her own personal tragedy would be. Would something happen to Grace, and make her parents cry all the time? Would her dad leave them like her friend Amy's dad did last summer and make her mom cry all the time? None of these things seemed likely. And so Ellie had figured it out – what would be the one thing that would make them all sad? What would ruin all of their lives?

The confirmation of her mother's impending death came in a most unusual way. The whole family was playing at a neighborhood park, and Ellie had taken off by herself to find a swing. The swings were her favorite; they made her feel like she was flying.

Her feet were almost touching the clouds when a small voice called from beside her. Ellie turned to her left and noticed a little girl about her age swinging right in sync with her.

"Hi, Ellie! I'm Jamie. How are you?" the little girl said with a smile. Ellie couldn't help but grin at this friend, but couldn't remember where they'd met.

"Do I know you, Jamie? I can't remember," she said and hoped that didn't sound rude.

"I come here a lot!" Jamie said as both girls continued to swing. "I'm sure I've seen you here before."

"Oh, great! Do you want to go play on the slide?" Ellie asked, thrilled to finally have a friend her age to play with. She wanted to show her off to Grace, who always had a gaggle of girls swirling around her. For a moment, Ellie almost forgot to be sad.

"Maybe in a minute, but I want to tell you something first," Jamie said, and both girls slowed their swinging. A few seconds later, they were sitting a few feet apart, suspended in air, and Ellie felt like the world had stopped.

"Sure, Jamie. What's up?"

Jamie smiled her beautiful, contagious grin and reached out for Ellie's hand.

"I wanted to tell you not to worry any more. Everything is going to be okay. When the time comes, you will be strong. And you will not be alone. Your dad and Grace will be there for you. Just remember, it will all be okay."

Ellie felt her smile instantly fall from her face, and she glared at the little girl.

"What are you talking about? How do you know—"

"Ellie! Time to eat!" Ellie turned to her mom's call, and it took her a few seconds to locate her family. Then, she saw them. They were sitting on a picnic blanket, a scrumptious lunch of peanut butter and banana sandwiches, potato chips, and lemonade spread out before them.

"I've got to go—" Ellie turned back to Jamie, to tell her she was leaving and that she was crazy, but the little girl was gone. Ellie scanned the entire park and could not find her.

Ellie ran to her family and settled in for their lunch, but the conversation never left her mind. And from that moment on, she waited for the day to come.

Now, as the carpool line continued in front of her, Ellie tried to distract herself and focus on something else. Ellie kept picturing her mom, and the thought of losing her would not go away. The fear was overwhelming. She could not imagine what she would do if her mom was gone. Who would help her get ready in the morning and put her favorite clip on the side of her hair, just the way she liked it? Who would fix her lunch every day and put little drawings on the napkins that made her smile? Who would pick her up every day right after recess, always on time?

Ellie found herself breathing faster and faster; she tried to calm herself but the worries would not stop. Who would fix their dinner and help her take a bath? Who would kiss her goodnight and touch her hair so softly until she slipped into her slumber? No one could do these things but her mom, and Ellie would be all alone soon.

Her sister, Grace, didn't seem to worry. Every time Ellie had tried to warn her, Grace had just laughed and run off with her friends or watched her favorite show on TV. Ellie supposed Grace didn't even really need a mom any more. She dressed herself and made her own lunch, so she would be just fine. But not Ellie; Ellie would have no one.

Ellie turned and looked at the car line once more. No sign of her mom. The knot in her stomach grew tighter and she could feel the tears starting to fall. She tried to hold them back because she knew the other kids were watching. Once she started crying, they would start laughing and making fun of her.

"Crybaby!" they would yell. "Little smelly Ellie is a big ol' baby!" She hated it when they teased her; she wanted to run and scream and yell back. But instead, she would close down; she would go to a corner of the room and she would imagine. She would pretend that she was a princess in a tall, white, glittery castle filled with white horses and surrounded by a beautiful ocean with leaping dolphins as far as her eyes could see. The castle would be full of friends and family, and they would love her forever – they would never make fun of her. And most importantly, her mom would be there, and they would never be separated again.

Ellie was caught between her tears and her imaginary world, desperately afraid that someone would notice, when a hand touched her back. Ellie looked up quickly.

"Mom! I knew you'd come—" she started, but the face before her was an unfamiliar one. The woman had graying hair and softly wrinkled skin. She smelled of banana nut muffins, Ellie's favorite.

"Hi Ellie, I'm Miss Gina. I'm here to wait with you until your family picks you up."

Ellie stared at the large woman who reminded her of her grandma. Did she know her?

"Hi, Miss Gina. Do you know when my mom will be here? She is never late to pick me up. She knows I get…nervous when she's not here."

Miss Gina just smiled slowly and rubbed Ellie's shoulder.

"Don't worry, Ellie. I know your family will be here soon. And no matter what, I am sure that your mom loves you, and she wouldn't want you to worry. Everything is going to be okay."

Ellie stared at the woman and tried to understand her words. Had she heard from her mom? Did she know she was on the way?

For some reason Ellie's stomach did settle down a bit and she sat a little closer to Miss Gina while she watched classmate after classmate get into their waiting cars. Her tears had faded and though she was still worried, she felt better with Miss Gina sitting beside her.

The carpool line moved on. Ellie noticed the mom in each car and the smile on her face as she picked up her child. It made her miss her own mom even more. She slowly fingered the silver bracelet on her right wrist. It was a charm bracelet, but it only had a single charm: a ballet shoe. Ellie had started taking ballet that year, and her mom was so proud. She said that every year, they would add a charm to that bracelet; it would be something special just between them. It was Ellie's most prized possession, and she held onto it tightly as she looked again for her mom's car.

When only a few kids were left in the carpool line, and Ellie was starting to get worried again, she heard someone calling her name.

She looked up and noticed her dad running towards her. His eyes were red and his hair was all ruffled, but Ellie had never been happier to see him in her whole life.

"Miss Gina, that's my dad. I can go now. Thanks for—" Ellie turned to thank the nice woman, but no one was there. Ellie supposed she had left to help another kid who was still waiting for their mom.

Without another thought, Ellie grabbed her backpack and ran to meet her father.

"Daddy, what's wrong? Where is Mommy? She's never late! I was so worried!" Ellie couldn't help herself from chastising him, but when she got closer, he fell to his knees.

He grabbed her tight around the shoulders and held her so close she couldn't breathe. She could feel his big arms shaking but he wasn't talking. As she held him close, she didn't notice her precious charm bracelet slipping from her hands, falling to the ground.

They were frozen there for a minute, and Ellie could see that a few of the teachers and the remaining students were watching her. At first, she was afraid they would make fun of her dad for acting so weird, but she saw quickly that there was no laughter in their eyes. Instead, and maybe even worse, they looked sad. The note in her backpack from her teacher suddenly felt like it weighed a hundred pounds. She knew she had been too happy. She had finally gone too far.

"Daddy, please," she begged, touching his hair as he cried. "What's wrong?"

She stood there for a minute more until her father finally rose to his feet. He took her hand, and they started walking towards the parking lot.

He didn't say anything, and she didn't ask any more. She knew.

4 / THE WELCOME

Juliet stood completely still, soaking in all that was around her. The first thing that struck her was the light which surrounded her and illuminated everything in sight. It seemed to radiate from one main source, high above where she stood. At least she thought she was standing.

Her new form was different than before; she still had arms and legs but she felt weightless, as if she could take off running at any moment and leap into the air, never to come down.

Juliet continued to gaze around her. Thousands and thousands of others filled the floor of the enormous stadium where she stood. This was bigger than any football game she'd ever seen. But the crowd that composed it was similar to one you might see at a large sporting event: young and old, from every race and nationality.

There were balloons everywhere, in all different sizes and colors. It was a rainbow assortment that included shades Juliet had never seen before. There were aisles upon aisles of chairs covering the entire arena, each one with a name neatly printed on the back of it.

As Juliet searched for her name, she saw a large elderly woman step to the front of the main stage that was suspended in the air in the midst of their chairs.

"Excuse me," she said, her soft voice amplified perfectly though no microphone equipment was being used.

A hush came upon the crowd and everyone began taking their seats.

"This way, Juliet," someone said and Juliet looked around for the source of the most angelic voice she had ever heard. Appropriately, it came from a being Juliet knew instantly to be an angel.

She was a tall creature, adorned with flowing amber hair and dressed all in white. On her back, tucked down but unmistakable, were two massive wings.

"I'm Avia, and I was your guardian on earth. We will have more time to talk later, but I wanted to say a quick hello and help you get situated," she said, and Juliet stared for a moment in awe. She was taken aback as the angel reached out to embrace her in a quick hug. Every word that came out of Avia's mouth was like a rain drop, so precise and delicate. Juliet had a million questions for her, including where she had been a bit earlier that morning, but Avia just smiled.

"Soon, we will get a chance to talk, and I will share many answers with you. For now, please have a seat and enjoy the show!" An instant later, Juliet was somehow at the seat with her name on it, and Avia had disappeared. She was disappointed to see her go, but she looked forward to their discussion. She had many, many questions.

Juliet sat down and continued to stare at this most curious scene around her. Could this really be happening?

"Welcome, everyone," the elderly woman on the main stage said beautifully, and Juliet was amazed to notice that everyone in the entire stadium had taken their seat.

"I am Elizabeth, and I will be your guide for the day. Many of you may not know where you are right now; some of you may have guessed. Please, let me be the first to say to you: Welcome to heaven!"

A loud murmur instantly covered her voice, and Juliet could see the elderly woman smile.

"I hope that did not come as too big of a shock. I cannot tell you how good it is to see you here. For the next little bit, a few of us will be welcoming you and letting you know what to expect. And then, the big show will begin."

Again, the murmuring overwhelmed the crowd. Juliet looked around her, to the man on her left and the child on her right. They did not return her looks of shock; they seemed to know exactly where they were.

"Hello, I'm Juliet," she said, first to the little girl on her right.

"Hi, Miss Juliet. It's nice to meet you. I'm Melanie and I am…I mean, I was 5."

Juliet smiled at her. Five years old, just like Ellie. A sudden pain gripped at Juliet's heart. *Ellie! And Grace and Mark! What were they doing right now? They must be so lost without her.* Juliet felt tears welling up in her eyes and noticed the little girl staring up at her.

"Why are you crying, Miss Juliet? Isn't this place beautiful? It's just like my mommy told me it would be."

"Of course, you're right, Melanie. I was just thinking of my family back on earth and how much I miss them already."

Melanie smiled. "I miss my family too, but we were ready. We had many, many days to prepare for this."

Juliet couldn't help but return the little girl's smile. She seemed so calm and so at peace here, while Juliet was a ball of confusion and worry. How could they both be in heaven? Was it okay to have such conflicting thoughts here? Juliet found herself reaching out to touch one of the little girl's long, blonde curls.

"Your hair is so pretty; did you get that from your mommy?"

Melanie grinned even brighter and reached out to grab her hair.

"I have hair? Are you sure?" She was so excited to feel it between her fingers. "It's been so long since I've had hair. Mommy didn't tell me it would come back in heaven, but I should have known!"

As the little girl continued to stroke her beautiful blonde hair, Juliet patted her softly on the back and then turned to the older man on her left. He looked to be about the same age as her father would have been, and she was instantly curious about how he had arrived here. She was about to ask him about his circumstances when a hush fell back over the crowd.

The woman who had welcomed them earlier still stood on the stage, and Juliet instantly worried that she had been ignoring her.

"I hope you have all gotten a little acquainted and feel a bit more at ease," she said kindly and smiled broadly at the crowd.

"Now I won't be the only one to tell you this, but I like to sneak it in when I can: Well done, everyone. As I said before, we are so happy to have you here, and we know you will be happy to be here. Don't worry if it takes awhile for everything to soak in. There will be a lot for you to learn in the next little bit, and really, for the rest of eternity," the old woman chuckled softly to herself, and Juliet felt a few of her nerves return.

The woman on stage looked behind her briefly and then addressed the crowd once again.

"I am proud to introduce to you someone that many of you already know of, but it is unlikely that any of you have ever met. He is today's guest speaker, and I know you will all be thrilled to meet him. Joseph, please come on up."

Collectively, the crowd leaned forward. Dressed in a long green robe, sandals, and sporting a beard that was likely popular in his day, a man stepped to the front of the stage.

As he began to speak, Juliet noticed that his words were perfect English, without the hint of an accent. She wondered if everyone automatically heard and spoke in their native tongue and made a mental note to inquire about it later. She then turned her attention to the biblical legend.

"Welcome again, everyone. This is the beginning of a wonderful journey for you. I know that some of you may still be a little nervous, a little uncertain about what is to come and about why you are here.

"Some of you may have been in the middle of something important; some of you may have just started your lives on earth. Some of you may have friends and family back home that you know won't make it without you. Many of you are probably questioning the timing of God's decision to bring you home at this specific time. You may wonder if He has made a mistake.

"Well, I am here to tell you that He does not make mistakes. He has a detailed plan that involves you and me and everyone you see here today...as well as everyone who has ever lived on earth or ever will live on earth. Only our omnipotent Creator could have put together all those pieces into such an intricate and beautiful puzzle.

"And though you may know Him and love Him and trust Him, you may wonder what His plan was with you and how it could possibly be a good thing that you are here among us today. Those are all fair questions and honest doubts. That is why I am here. I want to share with you my story and hopefully give you a little insight into that flawless plan of our Father."

Juliet sighed at his words. That had been a lot to take in, and she had to admit that she did question God's decision to end her life that day. She had two little girls and a husband to take care of; they really would be helpless without her. Mark didn't even know where she kept the checkbooks or how she filed the bills, let alone how to make dinner or do the laundry. Would her mom move in and help for awhile? She lived so far away and had never been close to the girls, something Juliet now regretted. Would they ever feel safe and loved again?

She thought of all the things she would miss: watching her daughters grow up, giving them advice through their teenage years, helping them pick out their homecoming dresses, seeing them at their weddings. She had left them right when they needed her most, something she had vowed would never happen. Her eyes stung with tears.

As she wiped them from her cheeks, Joseph continued.

"When I was born, I already had ten older brothers waiting for me. Most of the time, we got along, but many of them felt hostility towards me because I was born of my father's most treasured wife. At one point my father, who you will get to meet later on, tried to do something very kind for me. He made me the most amazing coat, comprised of threads from every color of the rainbow. It was a kind gesture, but it put into action a most hateful plan by some of my brothers. Perhaps I wore the coat too often or loved it too much. Whatever the case, my brothers seemed to grow angrier each time they saw it. This pushed their rage over the edge, and they decided that I could no longer be one of them.

"To make a long story a little shorter, I was working in the field one day, trying hard to prove my worth to my brothers, when everything went black. I awoke many hours later at the bottom of a pit. It was dark, muddy, and I waited and waited for someone to rescue me. But no one came.

"My brother Reuben would tell me later that he had planned to rescue me the next day, after my other brothers had calmed down. But he would never get that chance. From the bottom of the pit, I heard a rustling coming from high above. I called out as best as I could. I was confident my brothers had found me and were there to save me. But strangers stood at the top of the pit, and as I emerged on the rope they had thrown down, these burly men beat me in the face and made everything go black again.

"By the time I had awakened, I was in the midst of a caravan, jumbled about on the rear of a donkey. My head ached and my body felt weighed down. Tight ropes were wrapped painfully around my wrists and ankles, and as my entire self flailed helplessly about in the heat, I knew I was going to die."

Juliet's eyes were focused on Joseph. She had heard this tale many times as a child and had even listened to her children recite it when she picked them up from Sunday school. But to hear it from the man himself was amazing. So much trouble for such a young life. And she knew that there was more to come. She returned her attention to the historical figure as he continued his tale.

"As I prayed silently to God, over and over again, a peace came over me. It was a comforting realization that everything was going to be alright. We traveled for days, and by the time we reached our destination, my body ached all over. I was sure one or more of my ribs were broken and I was seriously beginning to doubt the reassuring peace I had felt a few days earlier. We were in another country now, some place I had never been. The air was still hot and the ground still dry, so in some ways, it felt like home. But the towering structures that stood stark across the horizon as we drew closer made it feel like another world entirely.

"Almost immediately I was taken to a large room where many other shackled men of all ages were gathering. A man with golden attire who appeared to be in charge looked directly at me and summoned me forward. He provided payment to my captors, and they shoved me away. I stumbled into the group of the selected. As I noticed the young and old about me, I wondered what our future would hold.

"I hope that I am not boring anyone," he said softly as he looked into the crowd. "I desperately want to show you that I understand many of you have come from hard circumstances and many of you doubt that anything you went through was for a reason. But it all was. Everything you survived brought you here today."

Juliet looked in the rows in front and in back of her. She noticed the diverse collection of individuals that were represented in just the fifty or so people directly around her. Children, grandparents, young women, men in their prime. Some were dressed in traditional American clothing, others bore the attire of their native lands. All were focused intently on the speaker.

"I will keep the rest of my tale brief," Joseph said with a smile that indicated his interpretation of *brief* may not have been the same as that of his audience. "I worked for endless days under the golden man, who was called Potiphar. I would later learn that he was one of the most powerful men in the land, subservient only to the great Pharaoh. Potiphar was a ruthless ruler, causing all of us to lift, pull, and build until our fingers bled and the skin on our feet had all but peeled away. But I never complained. One thing I had learned from being around all of my brothers: complaining was a sign of weakness and those in power did not appreciate whining. Though many around me grumbled without ceasing, I never mentioned a word of complaint.

"Apparently, this was noticed by Potiphar, and after a long time, I was promoted. I continued to work hard and eventually became a ruler in Potiphar's household. I thought that I had finally made it; this was the blessing God had in store for me. And then, when I was finally learning to enjoy the surplus and relax, a horrible event occurred. Potiphar's wife, one of the many women who he spent time with and the one with the most power, took a liking to me. She was a beautiful woman, and I would be lying if I said I did not note her pleasing appearance. But Potiphar had been so good to me that I could not betray his trust; I could not go behind his back.

"His wife, however, grew tired of waiting. When she finally had enough of my rejections, she made up a lie about me. I thought Potiphar would know there was no truth to her words, that he would be confident in my loyalty, but that wife of his was mesmerizing and demanded that I be punished.

"Once again, I was thrown into a deep, dark place. Days passed slowly, until one evening my cell was thrust open and two men were thrown inside. I recognized them instantly: the baker and cup bearer of the mighty ruler, Pharaoh. They both were trembling with fear and paced day and night, terrified they would be executed. One night, I had a dream about these men. Though the news was not all good, I felt compelled to tell these men their fates: the cup bearer would be forgiven, but alas the baker would not.

"My dream unfortunately came to pass, and not long after, my cell was empty again. Months went by, and I continued the hard labor and suffered through the inhumane living arrangements. I had once again almost given up hope when the cup bearer reappeared. He ordered the guards to get me out of prison and took me straight to Pharaoh. Pharaoh had been disturbed by a dream and needed my interpretation. God gave me the eyes to see, and I told him what I knew. Through my guidance, Pharaoh was able to properly harvest his crops during the abundant times and was prepared when a devastating drought came.

"Pharaoh never forgot that I was the one who gave him this knowledge, and soon I was appointed to a great position of leadership. Once again, I was given luxurious robes, my choice of residence, and plentiful amounts of food. I thought that God had restored everything to me, and then some.

"But the most amazing blessing was still to come. The horrible drought that I spoke of affected not only our land but all the surrounding ones as well. On a day that I will never forget, I was working in the high palace when I looked out the window and saw a large group coming from afar. I knew at once who it was – my family! My brothers!

"What a great reunion! In the end, my father also made the great journey from our homeland, and we were all together again. Pharaoh showed a deep kindness to us all and treated my family like royalty. It was a blessed time. But I will never forget the years I spent in prison, separated from all that I knew and loved. I often thought that God had left me to die, that he had turned His face from me. But, in the end, I was able to see that He never gave up on me. Every misstep I took, every tragedy that came my way, I could be sure that God was at work in the background, ensuring that all that I went through would be transformed into good.

"Some of you may not have seen the end of God's plan in your life. But you will all see very soon; everything will be made clear. Thank you all so much for listening today. I hope that my story has brought you some relief. Please feel free to talk amongst yourselves. We will have a brief pause and then Elizabeth will be back to announce your next speaker."

Juliet continued to stare at the stage for a few moments after Joseph left, unable to move or speak. She had just heard the most amazing words from one of the most riveting characters in the Bible. His words were inspiring and she began to wonder: what good did her death bring? How was it helpful to others? Though the thought of being apart from her family still made her ache inside, a small part of her was excited to know and to see what would come next. All of this was just the beginning!

As she waited for the next speech to begin, Juliet once again turned to the man on her left, ready to introduce herself.

"Hi, I'm Juliet," she said to the graying elderly man beside her. Though he was old, Juliet could clearly see that he was once a man of brawn and strength.

"Hello, Juliet. I'm Harold. How have you enjoyed our experience so far?"

Juliet looked closely at her new friend and saw that his face was soft and his eyes were sad, probably similar to hers, and she instantly knew he was missing someone.

"This is incredible," she said softly. "I only wish my family could share this with me. I wish I could tell them I am okay and that everything is going to work out somehow."

The old man looked at her.

"I know how you feel," he said, shifting his eyes to the floor. "I was so sure that I was ready to leave earth and come here, but when the time came, I don't think I left behind all the right words and directions for my family. I worry they will be lost without me. I had more that I needed to share. More that I needed to explain."

Juliet nodded. "I completely understand. I left two little girls and a man who has no idea how to turn on an oven or a washing machine! I am so afraid they will be helpless without me."

Harold laughed. "I never knew how to do those things either, until after Marge was gone. Then, I taught myself. Mostly I just threw everything into the laundry and it all came out just fine. Though nothing was ever quite wrinkle-free, the way Marge liked it."

Juliet smiled. "How many children did you have?"

"Thr-," he began and then stopped. "I had four children," he said with a sigh and a far away glance. Juliet knew he was thinking of them now, and she was trying to picture her family when their host, Elizabeth, returned to the stage.

"Thank you so much, Joseph, for those inspiring words. I know you have touched everyone here today. Now, we have another special speaker for you. He is a member of your graduating class and, like all of you, still in awe of being here today. But his feelings and experiences seem to mirror many of your own, which may ease your anxiety a little. Please welcome William, or Willy, as he was sometimes known, to the stage."

From the midst of the crowd, a man stood. He seemed to be a little surprised to hear his name called, and he shuffled quickly to the middle of the stadium. He wore denim pants and a button-down shirt, and Juliet could tell just by looking at him that he had been a hard worker all his life. He wasn't very old, probably her age, but his eyes looked older.

"Hello, everyone," Willy began slowly. They could all hear the shaking in his words. "I am honored and flat-out shocked to be speaking to you today. In fact, I am in complete shock to be here at all. The last thing I remember, I was flying high in the sky in the midst of a tornado, praying for a soft landing. I'm assuming God heard that prayer, but apparently he had a different idea." Willy laughed a little and the audience joined with him.

"I am not completely sure why I was chosen to speak to you today, but I have a feeling I need to share one experience with you. As I was ushered here today by angels, attempting to get my bearings and figure out exactly where in the world I landed, I heard a voice shouting at me. It was a very familiar voice. A voice I have heard shout many times before, but never in a way that would bring me joy.

"But this man calling my name ran to me with pure happiness and embraced me in a way that I did not know was possible. Today, as I entered heaven, I was greeted by my father. Apparently, he pushed through a few barriers and made it down from the stands to greet me."

Juliet looked up. She was not sure how she had not noticed it before, but she could now see that they were surrounded by thousands upon thousands of faces, rising into the clouds in the stands around them. They were all sitting silently, but a pure joy and peace shone from them.

"Soon, you will all get to meet this group of friends and family who are here cheering you on today. Apparently, I got in on that surprise a little earlier than most!"

Willy smiled into the stands and then continued. "For as long as I can remember, I have hated my father. He was a mean and abusive man to me and all of my family as we grew up. As soon as I was old enough, I moved out of the house and did not return until he had died. For the last few years of his life, I refused to speak to him.

"When he died, I did not know that he had turned his life around; I did not care. I was so bitter at him and all that he had done. I forgave him in my heart but chose never to speak with him again on earth. I couldn't bear it.

"But as soon as I saw him here, I was filled with a thankfulness and peace that he did not leave his life the way it had once been. He changed, and though he was not able to ease all of his hurts on earth, he has been praying for me ever since he got here. This is the same way you will pray for those that you love – and the way that those who went before you prayed for you."

Willy smiled and looked back at Elizabeth as if to indicate that he was finished. She rose, and he turned to step down and then abruptly turned back to the crowd.

"Oh, and one last thing: if there is someone that you think could never make it here, someone who you think is beyond God's grace, then it is time to think again. If God could save my Pop, He can save anybody. There is always hope."

Elizabeth was by Willy's side now and gave him a brief embrace.

"That was just perfect, Willy…exactly what we'd hoped you would say!"

Willy looked relieved and walked quickly back to his seat. Elizabeth turned to face the crowd.

"I hope that has given you a brief introduction into the heart and soul behind heaven. Now, it is time for the main event! Please, sit back in your seats and relax. This is going to take awhile – but I assure you no one will be bored. And, of course, we have all eternity!"

5 / ELLIE AT TEN

Ellie's tenth birthday came and went without much fanfare. No cake, no party, not many presents. Though Ellie's dad asked her every year what she wanted and what kind of special event they could plan, Ellie had no interest in celebrating. Besides, who would she invite to her party? She had no friends at school. Everyone thought she was weird; even the teachers still looked at her with curious and concerned eyes.

Ellie didn't care. She didn't care much about anything. All it meant was another year gone by and another year closer to seeing her mom in heaven. All the time in between was useless and she had no intention of allowing herself any type of joy ever again. If she did, who knows what would happen?

Sure, her father caught her smiling every once in awhile. But if she ever noticed him watching, the blank, expressionless stare would return. It wasn't as if she was angry anymore, but more like she just didn't care. About anything.

The night of her birthday, Ellie sat and looked out the window for a long time. She gazed into the heavens, up at the stars, and wondered if her mom could see her.

She even bowed her head a little and started to ask God about it, but she stopped herself. She had given up on God a long time ago. Five years ago, to be exact.

***

"Hey, Marti! Good to see you back! It's been awhile!" John, the old mail director, called out with a wave to the substitute mail carrier he only saw every few months. Somehow, she always appeared when they needed her.

"Good to be back, John! It's nice to see your old face," she said with a grin. John chuckled. He liked this Marti; there was just something about her that brightened his day.

"Know what route you've got today?" he asked.

"I think the North Henderson area," she said with a small smile.

"I think you're right. Nancy is actually out today, so you'll be taking her route. Her daughter called up out of the blue and she's taking a personal day. First day she's taken off in months; first time she's heard from her daughter in years," John said, shifting through the papers on his desk.

"Imagine that," Marti said with a wave. Then, she gathered her supplies and directions and headed out in the little white mail truck she'd grown accustomed to over the years. She knew a much more efficient way to travel, but that wouldn't do here on earth.

Marti sorted through the mail as she headed off. She did her route quickly and accurately, but finally she found a letter that she had been looking for. She smiled a little as she tucked it into a stack of magazines and began her route, anxious to get to the work at hand. And she wasn't thinking about mail delivery.

***

Susie Montgomery picked up the mail off her entryway floor as she walked in.

"Bill, bill, bill…hmmm," she paused as she came to a letter addressed to an Ellie Mathews on Willow Street. The name was not familiar but she recognized the street. It was only a couple of blocks away. At that moment, her daughter Laynie stomped into the kitchen.

"What's for dinner?" she asked, her eyes glued to the floor.

"Hey, love. It's nice that you're talking to me again. I've been missing that beautiful voice of yours."

Laynie didn't return her mother's smile. "I'm just hungry," she said. "It doesn't mean that I've forgiven you."

Her mom sighed. Of course not; that would be too easy.

"Fine, take this letter down the street to Willow. I think it's the first brown house on the left. I've seen some bicycles out there; you never know, maybe you'll actually make a new friend."

"Yeah, right," Laynie said, grabbing the letter and storming off.

Again, her mom sighed and said another silent prayer. *Please Lord, let her make new friends. Maybe then she'll forgive me.*

When Laynie arrived at 741 Willow Street, she did in fact notice two bikes on the front porch. They both appeared to belong to young girls, though one looked brand new, as though it had never been used. Maybe this was a good chance for her to make some friends. Since moving here from California three weeks ago, she hadn't met anyone, though that would've been hard to do from inside her bedroom. She had stayed holed up in there most of the day and night, refusing to show her mom any sign of acceptance of this new place.

She would never forgive her mom for making them move halfway across the country. She'd lost all of her friends; she'd lost her horse and the ranch that she'd loved; and most importantly, she had lost her father.

Even though he wasn't dead, ever since their divorce was final, her mom had been adamant on getting as far away from him as possible. Even if that meant taking away all of Laynie's happiness.

Laynie didn't even know why her parents had divorced. It wasn't as if her dad hit her mom or anything. He didn't even treat them mean at all. He was away a lot, but Laynie knew he had an important job and he had to travel. She had accepted that ever since she was a little girl.

All Laynie knew was that one day she had come home from school and found boxes all over the living room and den. Her stuff had been packed and her mom's stuff had been packed, and there was no discussing it. Her mom said she would explain everything one day, and she had to trust her. But Laynie would never trust her mom again; she had ruined her life.

With a determined stride, Laynie approached the front door and knocked. She waited a few seconds and was about to just leave the letter on the porch when a movement inside caught her eye.

Laynie looked at the large window to the right of the door and met the gaze of a girl about her age. Neither of them smiled. Slowly, the girl walked to the door and opened it.

"Yes?"

"I have a letter for someone who lives here. It got delivered to our house by mistake," Laynie said.

Ellie reached out and took the letter. It was addressed to her and she couldn't hide her surprise. Who would mail her a letter?

"You look like you've never gotten a letter in the mail in your entire life," Laynie said with a smile.

Ellie kept looking at the letter.

"I never get anything in the mail," she said softly. "It's not like I have any..." she left that last part unsaid but Laynie understood.

"I don't have any friends either. My mom made us move to this stupid place and I hate it. No offense," she added at the end.

Ellie smiled. "I hate it too. Want to come in?"

***

Susie glanced at her watch and realized suddenly that Laynie had been gone for almost an hour. How had she let the time get away from her? Maybe Laynie was right; she was a horrible mom. What kind of parent would allow their child go to a stranger's house and then not worry every second until she returned home?

Susie had a lot on her mind, like how they would pay the mortgage next month, but that was no excuse. Her daughter should be her top priority at all times; that was why she had insisted they move all the way out here. Wasn't it? It wasn't just for selfish reasons; it wasn't just because she couldn't bear the thought of seeing her husband, her *ex*-husband, around town with another woman. She was doing this all for Laynie.

Susie was still trying to convince herself of that as she ran out the door. She was in an all-out sprint by the time she got to the Mathews' home.

She banged on the door and then knocked again, harder this time, when no one answered. She was about to try the handle herself when the door swung open.

A man about her age stood there and welcomed her inside.

"You must be Laynie's mom. We've been waiting for you," he said with a smile. Susie walked in to find her daughter sitting at the table with two other girls. They were all smiling.

Susie felt a mixture of relief and confusion. She realized she hadn't seen her daughter smile in what felt like months.

She sat down at the table.

"Do you like spaghetti and meatballs?" the man asked. "It's my specialty."

"It's the only thing he knows how to cook!" one of the girls said and everyone laughed.

"Yes, please," Susie said and tried to soak in the scene.

She looked at the man again, and he returned her gaze. There was a kindness in eyes but also something else. What was it?

As she took a plate of spaghetti, she realized what it was: sadness with a touch of loneliness. She knew that look well.

6 / THE WAITING AND WATCHING

Juliet sat on the edge of her seat; she couldn't wait for the main event to begin. At the same time, she was a bit nervous. What would it entail? A moment later, her questions were answered.

The bright light that illuminated their entire space began to descend towards the middle of the stadium. Somehow, the light grew closer to them, yet still continued to light every corner of heaven. For a moment, it blinded them all and many hid their eyes. But slowly, their sight adjusted and they were able to see a figure still bathed in light. He began to speak.

"I am so happy to see each of you. Welcome home!" He said. Juliet could not believe it. Was this who she thought it was?

"It is time for us to celebrate your life on earth and the life that is to come. Together, we will take a look back at all you did with your time there and with the gifts that I gave you. We will rejoice in your successes."

Juliet felt the excitement returning. She remembered all those years of Sunday school she taught, all of those donations to the charities she had given, all of the mornings she had spent on her knees praying. Surely, this would bring rewards here in heaven.

He continued, "We will then take a look at your life as I had planned it. You will clearly see all of the opportunities I gave you and how things could have been different. Some of you may be sad when you see this, but please know that I am still proud of you. We will sit together, and I will wipe away any tears that may fall. There is no reason to be upset or feel regret; there is no way to change anything that has happened. And there is no need to. You will see how we put things in place to pick up any slack or indecision on your part that caused the original plans to be changed."

Juliet sat back in her chair and felt the excitement melting away. A deep dread replaced it; would all of her mistakes really be paraded about in front of all of these people? This didn't sound much like the heaven she had dreamed of. All of her sins, all of her missed opportunities – she could think of countless more times when she had been wrong than when she had been right.

As she felt her face starting to turn red and the burn of tears in her eyes, the man beside her took her hand.

"It'll be okay; we've all made mistakes. We're all in this together," Harold said, and as he squeezed her hand, she knew he understood. He had made his own errors in judgment, the same as everyone in the entire stadium. But Juliet wondered if he'd messed up as many times as she had.

Juliet tried to smile back but she still felt the anxiety in her heart. He didn't know what she had done. But soon, everyone would. This thought made her feel ill and she was scanning the arena for any exits when He continued.

"As I begin calling names, the rest of you may join in the celebration or you may enjoy this time for fellowship. I believe the angels will be by to visit, and you can also use your viewing screen to take a peek at earth. You may be surprised to see how much time has passed there! Shall we begin? Alison Alvarez, please start your walk. The screen beside me will begin showing your life."

Juliet couldn't bear to watch. The massive screen near the main stage was playing images and video of baby Alison as she grew up. But Juliet didn't want to view any mistakes others had made. It made her too uncomfortable.

So, she turned to her new friend beside her.

"How do these viewing screens work?" she asked Harold. He already appeared to be taking a look at what was going on down on earth. Harold began to grin, and as she leaned over his shoulder, Juliet couldn't help but join him as they watched two little girls running around outside in a large yard, giggling as water sprayed on them from a sprinkler. Their little laughs could be heard softly from the viewing screen.

"My grandchildren…that's what I miss the most," he said quietly. Juliet saw a woman enter the picture. She scooped up the girls in a large towel and began to dry them off.

"That must be your daughter," Juliet said, and she could see the pride in the man's eyes.

"Yes, she is a busy lawyer with a hectic schedule, and yet she still makes time for her family. That is one thing I made sure that I taught my kids, mostly by my mistakes."

And then a man entered the screen and Juliet felt Harold shift in his chair and lean forward. The man and the woman on the screen smiled at each other; then more families approached and everyone sat together at a large table in the yard.

"That must be him," Harold whispered and Juliet noticed a tear streaming down his face.

"It seems like a family reunion," Juliet commented softly. The man nodded. He did not tell her that this was the child he had hidden from the rest, a result of a mistake he had made long ago. His wife had forgiven him and loved him still, but she had insisted that there be no contact with this other family. And he had agreed. From then on, he was the model father, but he could never forget the son he had left fatherless. Apparently though, his family was much more accepting than he had thought, and suddenly he ached for the loss of love and memories unrealized.

Harold seemed deeply engrossed in his thoughts, and Juliet resisted the urge to ask him more. From her vantage point, he didn't have anything to worry about. He sounded like the perfect father, the perfect man. He would have nothing to be anxious about when his turn approached and his decisions were revealed.

"I'm far from perfect, Juliet," Harold said with a laugh as he peeled his eyes from the screen and turned to face her. "For the first twenty years of my marriage, I was an awful husband, dad, and man. I have much to be ashamed of."

Juliet was embarrassed by the relief she felt at his faults. "But yet you're not worried at all about what everyone will think of you. I don't understand."

The man just smiled. "There's nothing I can do about it now. We've made it to heaven; there's no one that can take that away from us. It's important to see what I've done…the good and the bad. And I am interested to see what He had planned…and where I missed those gentle nudgings."

Juliet nodded, but she still wasn't sure. The thought of her lies, her deceits, her gossiping, her mistakes being broadcast for thousands to see did not make her feel good at all.

"Okay, well, show me how this thing works," she said, suddenly eager to distract herself.

The man held up the viewing screen, which was so thin it was almost weightless. It had the clearest and most lifelike picture she had ever seen; the images seemed to jump right off the screen. It was like they were right there, experiencing everything again.

"It's simple actually. All you have to do is think of a person or place, and it will automatically take you to that point in earth's present time. I've also discovered that you can think of a past time or place, and you can view that as well. I'm thinking about going back and viewing my funeral; I'm actually curious to see who showed up to the thing."

Juliet was amazed. "Thank you!" she said and held her viewing screen tightly. She instantly thought of Mark and the girls. The next moment, an image appeared on the screen. They were at a dinner table that Juliet didn't recognize. Mark was there, looking much the same but with some gray sprinkled in his hair. There was Grace, chatting away as she scooped mashed potatoes on the plate. Same beautiful green eyes and light blonde hair as her father, but there was a maturity to her face that made Juliet's heart leap. How old was she now? Definitely a teenager. Did she have questions about boys, about makeup, about friends who could say the meanest of things but be your closest confidante a minute later? Juliet felt the tears rising up as she noticed another girl at the table. Still quiet, still observing, her beautiful Ellie also seemed to be quite the same. Her dark hair ran past her shoulders and Juliet looked for that sadness in her eyes, that anticipation of something bad. But she did not see it. Instead, there was – Juliet couldn't believe it – a contentment. Almost happiness. She noticed that Ellie appeared to be looking at someone or something, and Juliet strained to see another figure just out of the picture. She was trying to look closer when the little girl beside her tugged at her arm.

"Yes, Melanie," she said, reluctantly peeling her eyes away from the screen and turning to her right.

"Look, Juliet! I am watching my own funeral. I wanted to see if my mommy and daddy were sad or if they were celebrating, like they promised me they would. They said they wouldn't cry, but they would be happy because they knew I was in heaven and all my pain was gone."

Juliet watched the screen with Melanie. The funeral had been held in a beautiful church with light streaming in through two large stained glass windows behind the altar. The entire facility was full; there was not an empty seat available. Juliet noticed a group of young girls sitting near the front. She assumed that they were members of Melanie's class, and she instantly wondered how Ellie had been at her funeral. She was anxious to take a look but forced herself to watch with Melanie.

A pastor stood at the front and began to speak.

"Welcome, everyone, to this most joyous occasion," he said with a big smile. Juliet was startled. Had the man forgotten where he was?

"In most cases, I realize, a funeral is a sad event, but we have all made a promise to our guest of honor that we will not cry today. Instead, we will rejoice with her because we know she is in a better place," he said and paused to look heavenward.

Melanie giggled a little in her seat. "Yep, they all promised me. I was so tired of the crying; so much sadness! I wanted to know for sure that my mom would be happy one more time because of me."

The pastor continued speaking, quoting appropriate scriptures and leading the crowd in a beautiful hymn. He was about to begin his eulogy, when a woman stood up from the crowd. She had been sitting in the front row, and Juliet noticed she had the same flowing blonde hair as Melanie. She knew instantly that it was her mother. Juliet also saw the tear-streaked cheeks and red eyes as the woman turned and fled the sanctuary.

"Oh no," Melanie gasped. "She promised." Juliet could see the devastation in the little girl's face as they watched. The screen followed the woman into the foyer where she knelt in a corner and let her sobs flow freely. A man came close behind. He put a hand on her back as she cried.

"Faye, I know this is hard, but remember, we promised her…we told her we would be happy for her."

The woman looked up and faced her husband.

"How can I be happy when I will never see the beautiful smile of my daughter again – when I will never get to hear her sweet laugh? I will never again hold her in my arms or feel her squeeze me back. You tell me how I can celebrate that!" There was anger in her words, but as she collapsed into her husband's arms, Juliet could tell it was mostly sadness.

As he slowly stroked her hair, Faye's husband responded: "Because you will see her smile again, and you will hear her laugh, and you will most definitely hold her in your arms while she squeezes you tight. We just have to wait a little longer and be comforted by the fact that our daughter is no longer in pain. She is no longer nauseous all day long and in agony all night. She is in a glorious place, and I bet she is watching down on us now."

Suddenly, Melanie's mom stood up. She looked up and it was if she was staring straight into heaven at Melanie.

"Do you think so?" she asked. "Melanie, if you can hear me, I love you! I miss you and I can't wait to see you soon. But until then, I will live here and make you proud. And then one day, we will be together again." Her voice shook a little at the end, and Juliet thought she might begin to cry again. But instead, she took a Kleenex from her pocket and wiped her tears away. Then she smiled a gorgeous smile of a woman at peace and looked again into the heavens.

"I love you, Melanie," she said once more. Then, with her husband by her side, she walked back into the service.

Melanie sighed, and Juliet saw the relief in her young eyes. Juliet waited a moment more, and when she was sure Melanie was okay, she turned back to her own viewing screen. She was unable to resist the temptation any longer. For a moment, she simply envisioned herself lying motionless in a casket at their church and a second later, images filled the screen.

Juliet's eyes were drawn to her husband and two daughters in the front row. Grace cried softly throughout the entire service, and Mark softly patted her back every few minutes. Ellie sat on the end, her face without expression. She did not cry; she did not look sad. She simply stared straight ahead.

This hurt Juliet more than Grace's tears. Her daughter seemed to be freezing up inside; she had always been a little distant, but now…Juliet could feel her heart tighten. This could devastate Ellie past the point of recovery; this could destroy her little girl's life.

With tears in her eyes, Juliet glanced around the small church. She recognized friends from high school, family members she hadn't talked to in years, and members of their congregation. There were also several people she didn't recognize and Juliet struggled to place them. Specifically, she saw a family at the back of the church – a man and his wife and their young son. She thought she recognized the mother as one of her fellow nurses from the hospital, but she only saw her for a second and couldn't be sure. The boy seemed to be about

Ellie's age. The couple occasionally whispered back and forth, and Juliet noticed that the father looked upset, like he didn't want to be there. She tried to look closer, to remember him, but she couldn't. She looked again at the little boy; his piercing blue eyes were the most beautiful she had ever seen. He looked around the church and scooted as close to his dad as he could, until he was almost in his lap. This seemed to irritate his father who took him firmly by the shoulders and sat him back in his seat. Juliet felt so sorry for the little boy with the beautiful blue eyes.

Suddenly, the church began to sing one of her favorite hymns. It talked about a happy morning when they'd all fly away to heaven, but Juliet had never really thought about the meaning behind the words. She had always loved the harmony and simple lyrics that lifted her spirits. Now, it was still unbelievable to her that she was living that song. Her life on earth was over; she had flown away – but was she glad?

She looked back to her emotionless Ellie and felt the common painful yearning of motherhood: all you want to do is keep your children safe and make sure they are happy. Now, she had no control over either of those things.

"Oh, but you do," the raindrop voice said behind her. Juliet turned back to see Avia standing there.

"Avia, I am so excited to talk to you," she said, setting the viewing screen in her lap and turning her focus to the angel. She hoped Avia had answers for her.

"And I can't wait to talk with you. There is so much to share. But first, I want you to know that you do have some control over your family, over what happens down on earth."

Juliet was shocked. "How?" she asked. "What can I do?"

"Well, you can do the same thing in heaven that you did down on earth: you can pray."

For a moment, Juliet almost said, "Oh, is that all?" but she held back her inconsiderate reply.

"Prayer is the most powerful weapon that you have, and it always has been. When you pray, you talk directly to God. And as it aligns with His will, it will be done at the proper time. You will soon see that there was no specific script for your life. No list of words you had to say or jobs you had to complete or a specific person you had to marry. There were just certain goals that you needed to accomplish. God left all the details up to you."

"That sounds so simple, Avia. But on earth, it didn't work that way. It wasn't as straightforward."

"It was that simple, but it was hard to fully understand because you couldn't see the whole picture. If something didn't happen exactly as you prayed it would, then it wasn't a part of God's plan in some way – or would have gone against God's plan. Some things that seemed so wonderful and necessary at the time may not have had the result that you intended or may have affected someone else in an extremely negative way. We are constantly updating the details and readjusting based on human choices and earthly occurrences. Somehow with His guidance, everything works out as it should, just not as you may have envisioned."

Juliet sat for a moment without speaking, and as she opened her mouth to rebut, Avia continued.

"You might ask how can healing a sick child or protecting a mother as she drives in her car could possibly go against God's plan, and those are very fair questions. We will spend a lot of time looking into that together, and though we can't fully go through it now, I want to give you two thoughts to consider. First, the bad things in life that happen aren't from God; they aren't a punishment or a test. They are simply a side effect of being human and living on earth. And that is not said to minimize the pain you went through or to trivialize the horrible tragedies that occur in any way. It is just to say that a part of living on earth is experiencing the random and at times inexplicable events that occur there. Also, Juliet, your time on earth and everything that you experienced there was just a tiny, tiny tip of the iceberg of your existence. The things that you went through and survived and even the events that eventually brought you here were just a training ground. The good that you experienced there was just a taste of the eternal joy you will live in here; and the pain that you felt, even those things that broke your heart in a thousand pieces, will only make your time here, in comparison, more amazing. The imperfection of earth will allow you to truly appreciate the completeness here in heaven."

Juliet nodded, accepting those statements for now with the express intent to press for more clarity later.

"Were people praying for me?" Juliet asked, looking into the crowd. She couldn't wait for the chance to meet with her family and friends. There was so much to discuss.

"Of course. Remember on your honeymoon when you and Mark had to stop at that gas station late at night? You were in the middle of a city you did not know, in an area that you were not familiar with. That gas station had actually been robbed four times in the past nine months, and the thieves were on their way back for more. It had been a successful job for them, a place where they could count on taking easy money. They were a little nervous that some security had been added, so this time they all brought guns. The robbery that night was going to turn out very ugly. But we were aware of it, and your family had prayed intently for your safety on the trip. Your dad here in heaven had been consistently praying for you; he had been proud to see you married and spent much time in prayers over you. God heard those requests, and sent me and four others to intercede. We stood guard outside that gas station all night. You did not see us when you went in, but as the thieves approached a few minutes behind you, we were all they could see. Five massive creature standing in front of the entrance. Even with their guns, they did not dare enter. And so they went home that night, and some of them never stole anything ever again. We tend to have that kind of effect on people," Avia said with a smile.

Juliet remembered that night clearly. She and Mark had been in the middle of their road trip, a honeymoon they thought was wonderful despite their lack of funds. One night, they had been lost and out of gas, and though the thought of stopping in an unknown area in the middle of the night did not appeal to them, they had no choice but to stop. Juliet honestly hadn't thought of it again, but now she could see clearly.

As much as that story touched her, it was the mention of her father that caught her off guard. He was here? Juliet wasn't sure if she wanted to see him or not; though she had made an outward peace with her father and forgiven him for his betrayal, she couldn't quite imagine talking to him for more than a few polite minutes or hugging him or telling him thank you for his prayers. He had left them high and dry; he had devastated her mother. And though he had apparently been granted forgiveness for those mistakes, Juliet actually didn't feel like she could have a relationship with him. She didn't have one with him on earth, so she wasn't sure how things could be different here in heaven. She made a mental note to talk with Avia about those feelings later; the angel was already excitedly continuing on with another example of the power of prayer.

"And do you remember the night before Ellie was born? You were still working because it was a month before your due date. You were out on a deserted road, doing one of your home health visits, when your car broke down. There wasn't another car around for miles. And then, your contractions began. At first you didn't really think the baby was coming, but when the contractions started coming six minutes apart, you panicked. You jumped out of your car and screamed for help, but there was no one to hear you. However, Someone up here heard you. And He sent your very own taxi ride to the hospital. Didn't you ever wonder what a taxi was doing out on that road?"

Juliet laughed. "You know, I never questioned it. I was just so thankful for my miracle that I never stopped to think that it really was one."

Avia smiled. "And there are countless more instances like that from your life on earth. It will be fun to reveal them to you!"

"So that was all because I had people praying for me? God's protection is based on the prayers of others?"

"Oh no, God's decisions are based on His will. But He listens to the prayers of His people and we are constantly sent to earth to do His bidding."

Juliet had so much to ask of her angel guide. So many times when she had wondered if there had been someone there, helping her and guiding her. She knew that they had eternity to discuss it all, but she was impatient.

"So, here in heaven, I will continue to pray for my family on earth?" Juliet asked.

"Yes," said Avia. "You will pray for them, and your prayers go straight to God. Then, in most cases, he sends one or more of us to help carry out the plan. Humans are amazing, resilient creatures but everyone can benefit from a little supernatural assistance now and then. In fact, though I'm sure you know this, you can be assured that all of your prayers on earth were heard as well. Throughout her young life, many angels were sent to try and comfort, prepare, and relieve Ellie. I know she is your greatest worry, and though she still remains a challenge, He has something planned for her that has been in the works for a long time."

Juliet looked at the angel. At the mention of her daughter's name, Juliet's heart ached. And to hear that she was in some sort of danger made Juliet sick with worry. She would continue to pray for her here in heaven but she knew she would be more effective as part of her life on earth. This brought up her most pressing question.

"Avia, can you tell me then how my car wreck – how taking me from my family – was part of God's plan?"

Avia smiled. "Of course. We are running out of time now, but we will absolutely discuss this more later. It is almost your turn to walk."

Juliet instantly turned her ear to the main stage as the next name was called.

"Nathan Marks, please come forward."

Juliet swallowed and closed her eyes.

"Don't be afraid, Juliet. It will all be okay. We are so proud of you for being here. This process is only to give you the full knowledge that you will receive as you review your life as it was lived and the life that was meant to be. Everyone goes through this together, and it will make you completely aware."

"But I don't want to be aware – I don't want to see all the opportunities I missed. I don't want to know about all of the lives that I could have changed. I just want to forget all of that and move on."

Avia smiled again. Was this angel always happy?

"I understand, Juliet. Completely. But to move on, you must reconcile your past. Only then can you truly move forward into purity and perfection – and soon, live in our pure heaven."

"I thought we were in heaven," Juliet said, a little confused now.

"You are – but there is more to come. So much more."

Juliet listened again to the names being called from the stage. It was almost her turn. Avia patted her shoulder.

"I will be back soon, and we will talk!"

Juliet nodded and was amazed to see Avia spread her wings and in one powerful motion, soar into the sky and disappear. The streak of light was blinding and Juliet covered her eyes.

She then turned back to her viewing screen. Until her name was called, she wanted to spend this time with her family. She thought of them now, and she was instantly back in the dining room with them.

It seemed as though more time had passed down on earth but she wasn't sure how much. They were wearing different clothes now, but the girls still seemed to be teenagers. Mark still had the sprinkling of gray in his hair but now it seemed a little more pronounced.

Mark and the girls were sitting and eating and Juliet strained to see what was on the table. Was it his famous spaghetti and meatballs? Juliet giggled as she remembered him making that for her on one of their first dates. She had been so impressed, and when he made it again a few weeks later, he shyly confessed it was the one and only dish that he knew how to make.

But that night's dinner seemed to be more complex. There were chicken and mashed potatoes; Juliet noticed a salad and fresh bread. They were all using napkins and of course dinnerware that Juliet didn't recognize.

Juliet then noticed another girl at the table. She seemed to be about Ellie's age and they were talking and smiling and laughing. It soothed Juliet's heart to see her daughter happy. Maybe this was a friend from school; Ellie had never brought home a friend before. Maybe they weren't so lost without her. Maybe Avia was right; maybe everything would turn out okay. A moment later, the girl turned towards Grace and began to talk with her. Juliet saw Ellie's face fall and turn back to the familiar blank stare.

And then Juliet noticed something else: one more place at the table. Her heart stopped for a moment, and she thought about turning away, but her curiosity wouldn't let her. A moment later, a woman entered the screen. She was of average height and build with light brown hair and a kind face. She paused for a moment by Mark's side and filled his glass with iced tea. His favorite. Juliet cringed as she saw him touch her back and look up at her. Her heart stopped as she saw the look in his eyes. She had seen that look often during their time together and, in fact, thought it had been reserved only for her. It was a look of love.

7 / ELLIE AT FIFTEEN

The day Ellie had been dreading for several years now was fast approaching. Most of the kids her age were beyond anxious for their birthdays to arrive so they could race to the DMV and claim their ticket to freedom: their driver's license. Ellie had even heard of some kids camping out the night before so that they could be first in line to receive the coveted card. Her feelings toward this step away from adolescence and into adulthood could not be more different.

Ellie felt a little guilty because she knew her father was excited about this landmark birthday. He had been talking about it for weeks now, and although he thought it was a surprise, Ellie knew he was also planning to take her to buy her first car right after they got the license. Not a new car, but a car. One that would be her very own.

Ellie had heard him telling Susan about it one night during their talks. She eavesdropped on these discussions often, and most of the time, she didn't mind what she heard. Susan was a kind woman, though Ellie would never call her mom. In fact, she still called her Susan while everyone else in the house called her Susie. It was just her little way of saying that she needed her space and didn't want to get too close. And no one would ever replace her mom.

That didn't seem to bother Susan; she still treated Ellie with patience and respect, always making sure she was included whenever Laynie and Grace wanted to go to the mall or get their nails done. Though Laynie had been more Ellie's friend when their families first met, as the years went by, she grew closer and closer to Grace. They liked to do more of the same things, and when Laynie's anger and resentment toward her mom faded and eventually disappeared, Ellie couldn't relate to her as well as she used to. She tried, really she did, but eventually Laynie would always end up taking Grace's side or begging to hang out with Grace and her friends. And Grace seemed to love it. Laynie seemed to be the little sister she'd always wanted.

Ellie thought again about the new car. She was going to be expected to drive it and to love it; this was an extravagant gift from her father, one that she didn't want to seem unappreciative of. But how could she explain to him that the thought of driving her own car made her stomach queasy? How could she tell him that every day in driver's ed was torture – that she never volunteered to drive and only sat behind the wheel when she absolutely had to? How could she admit that, every time she drove, she'd sit alone in the car for several minutes after everyone had left, waiting for her heartbeat to slow down and the dizzy, weak feeling to leave? She hated driving; every time she gripped the steering wheel, she thought about her mom and the last time she had been driving. She thought about the fear her mom must have felt and the pain. She knew all the statistics on driving; car accidents were the leading cause of death for kids her age. Maybe it was her destiny…to die just like her mom. And sometimes that was a strangely comforting thought, but most of the time, she was scared to die.

She couldn't shake these thoughts and felt tears stinging her eyes when Laynie bounced into the room they shared. She flopped onto the bed beside Ellie and smiled.

"Getting ready for the big day?" she asked. Laynie's family had always gone all out when celebrating birthdays. Since her mom had left, Ellie and her father and sister had not been so quick to celebrate, though some years Ellie's dad had gone overboard trying to compensate.

"I guess," she said and tried to look a little interested. She desperately missed Laynie's friendship and wished she wasn't always running off with Grace.

"Are you sure you don't want a party? We could invite all of our friends from school and all of the popular kids. Your dad said you could do whatever you wanted," Laynie said, and Ellie could tell she was excited about any reason to throw a big party and impress their classmates.

"It's just not my thing," Ellie said, but knew Laynie wouldn't understand.

Laynie just sighed and stood up slowly. "I know, I know. But eventually, you're going to have figure out what your thing is. You can't just go through life without having any fun and with nothing to live for. You just mope around all the time and never do anything. I mean, you might as well be—"

Laynie stopped and Ellie could see her eyes grow wide.

"I didn't mean that, Ellie. I just—"

"It's okay. Why don't you just go find Grace?" Ellie asked and instantly regretted the anger in her voice.

Laynie looked at her for a moment more and left the room. Ellie didn't go after her.

Better to let her go. There was no need to get close to someone else who, at any moment, could be out of her life forever.

***

The night before her sixteenth birthday, Ellie went to her favorite place in the world. It was the only place where she could look sad and no one would question her. It was the only place where everyone else looked the way she felt, and she didn't have to secretly resent anyone's happiness. At the cemetery, she felt at home. Next to her mom's grave, she felt no judgment.

Today, Ellie desperately wanted a sign from her mom. She needed something to tell her that it was going to be alright. She would soon be driving to school every day; Laynie would make sure of that. She was a few months younger than Ellie and couldn't wait to be off the bus. Since Grace went early for volleyball practice in the fall and basketball in the spring, she couldn't drive them. Laynie was sure this would elevate their status at school; Ellie was just hoping she could somehow avoid looking like a petrified freak in front of her peers.

As she knelt there amongst the weeping willows and swaying oak trees, she gently touched the granite of her mom's tombstone. Slowly, she read the words she had memorized many years ago.

Juliet Mathews
Beloved wife and mother
April 7, 1953 – May 14, 1988
…All things work together for good to them that love God.
-- Romans 8:28

Ellie hated that quote. Her dad had chosen it, and she had never understood why. Several times, he had tried to talk to her, to tell her that he believed her mother was taken for a reason – that God needed her up in heaven and knew they would survive here on earth, but Ellie couldn't have disagreed more.

The day her mom died was even worse than Ellie had imagined. When her dad told her the news, it never quite sunk in, and Ellie kept thinking her mom would come home. Every day in carpool line, she would still look for their car, though it had long ago been towed away to a junkyard. Every night, she pictured her mom coming in to tuck her in; she almost felt the soft touch of her mom's hand against her cheek and the gentle brush of a kiss on her forehead. Almost.

Each time she remembered that her mom was not coming home, it was like a sharp knife digging away at her heart. Somehow, the pain never lessened; her insides stayed raw and vulnerable, and she didn't think they would ever heal.

Today, at the cemetery, all she really needed was a sign…something that told her to keep going and to keep trying…that eventually it would all get better.

She almost looked up to heaven, almost whispered a prayer, but she still couldn't bear that. She couldn't stand the thought of giving in, even just a little, to the One who had taken everything away from her.

She stayed at the gravestone a few more minutes, and then slowly stood. She laid a single rose on the ground and blew a kiss to her mom. As she turned to leave, her foot nudged against something on the ground, but she didn't stop to look at it. She just shook whatever it was from her foot and kept walking.

As she walked home, Ellie didn't notice the figure approaching the spot where she had just stood. She didn't see the man-like creature kneel to the ground and pick up something from the grass. She missed it when he placed the silver bracelet with the little ballet charm in his pocket.

He would have to try again later.

***

The day that Ellie got her license, everyone was excited except for her. Her dad was beaming and Ellie had to force herself to smile and look surprised when they drove to the used car lot after their stop at the DMV. She looked for the safest car they had, but none seemed to be the armored tank she was looking for.

Finally, they settled on a reasonably priced sedan in blue, her favorite color. After thanking her Dad profusely and ensuring that at least he was happy on this day, Ellie began the slow drive back home. She was glad she would have a few weeks to practice the route before school began.

If Ellie could have seen the highway through heavenly eyes, the sight would have amazed her. Silver streaks of light flashed by, unseen to humans, and faster than anything known to man. Angels covered the roadways at all times: so many people, so many dangers, so many prayers going up. At any one moment, angels were slightly edging cars back into their lanes, placing detours at strategic spots, and helping weary drivers stay awake.

On that day, if Ellie could have seen her own car, she would have known that her non-prayers were being answered and that her heart's desires were still being heard.

An army of angels surrounded that little blue sedan; tall, broad, and powerful creatures escorted her safely to her destination. And they would continue to do so each and every time Ellie set foot in the car. Her mom's prayers from heaven would ensure that.

8 / THE WALK

Juliet could feel tightness in her stomach and a weakness in her knees as her turn to walk to the main stage approached quickly. Part of her was still focused on what she had seen at home – Mark and her daughters with two new ladies in their lives. Overall, everyone looked happy, or at least no worse than when she had left. This left her both relieved and sad; maybe she hadn't been as integral to her family's well-being as she had thought. Was she about to see what a waste the rest of her life had been?

"It was no waste, Juliet. You made important contributions to countless people during your relatively short time on earth," the beautiful, familiar voice said.

Juliet looked up to see Avia standing behind her once again, as if she had sensed Juliet's increasing anxiety and returned to calm her down. Juliet was relieved to hear those words praising the good things she had done, but she was more focused on what she hadn't done. How many times had she missed a chance to say or do something that would make all the difference, that would change a life forever?

"Thank you, Avia, but I know that there are so many things that I should have done differently; so many mistakes that I made. I am terrified to face God as he reveals all of my failures."

"Juliet, God has already seen all of your failures, and He has already forgiven them. Today is not about being punished or embarrassed. Your eternity in heaven has already been given to you and cannot be taken away. Today, you will see all of the good that you did, and you will be rewarded for it."

Juliet slowly smiled; her heartbeat seemed to stop. Would it really be okay? She wanted to believe so desperately that this wouldn't be the most painful experience of her life. Or afterlife.

"Rewards? For what?"

"You will see. Now, please do not think this will be an easy experience. As you review your life, you will see things that you wish you would have done differently, and there will be regret as you see all that God had planned for you. But the most important thing is already established; today we look back once more to celebrate your time on earth and then to move forward into so much more that God has planned."

Juliet tried to relax. This wouldn't be easy, but it wouldn't be awful. To her, it seemed a lot like preparing for childbirth. It was definitely worth the pain, but during the process, she wished she could have been anywhere else but in that hospital delivery room. Especially since she had made a decision not to use any pain medication during the delivery. But as soon as the pain hit, all that planning and preparation went right out the window. She remembered crying out for an epidural three hours into Grace's delivery and receiving one thirty minutes later. She had felt disappointed in herself afterwards, and though everything had obviously turned out okay, she wondered how many times in life she had given up instead of pressing forward with her original plan, no matter how tough it turned out to be. She would soon find out.

"Danielle Mathers, please come forward."

The woman at the beginning of Juliet's row stood up. Juliet saw her slowly walk towards the main stage, and her life story began to play on the big screen. The images and voices were at times clear and vivid. Then, they would become blurry and hazy flashes of light. Danielle walked intently; she appeared to be about the same age as Juliet when she left earth.

Danielle's baby images showed a chubby-cheeked angel with the same curly brown hair that she had now. As a young girl, Danielle seemed so happy. In all of the pictures and video, she was smiling and playing with her parents and other children her age. Then one day, the images seemed to darken, and a tension could be felt throughout the stadium.

The crowd could see Danielle cleaning a home, over and over again. Sometimes, she would clean an area once, only to begin cleaning the same exact spot again. She saw Danielle's purse, full of hand cleaners and sanitizing wipes, which she clung to like a lifeline.

The next set of images showed Danielle driving. She would drive in one area of a neighborhood and then circle back, sometimes three or four times through the same area. Juliet could see Danielle's eyes squinting, desperately searching for something in her rearview mirror.

Many images showed Danielle crying. She would be alone in her room or sitting in the kitchen, and a deep pain would register on her face. Hopelessness; intense anxiety; a sense of nowhere to go and no one to help.

Juliet couldn't turn away as the images continued. She saw Danielle with two young children, both with the same brown hair as their mom. Danielle would hug them tight and watch them play. She watched every move they made and often ran to them, in the midst of their playing to grab their hands and wipe them clean. They would scream and Danielle would look around, keenly aware of the looks the other moms gave her. But she couldn't stop. The process repeated itself over and over again until neither Danielle nor her children could take any more, and they would leave. Danielle would take their hands as they cried and lead them away, not able to look up and face the disapproving stares around her.

The next set of images showed Danielle at home, hundreds of pills strewn about her bed, surrounding her. She looked at them, ready to take them, ready to end her misery and the misery of her family. One last time, she fell to her knees and cried out to God. She had given up all hope; there was no way out of this nightmare in her mind.

Suddenly, a little girl ran into the room. Danielle jumped in surprise and Juliet saw her stand up and turn away from the bed. The little girl hugged her mother's feet and kissed at her toes.

"I need you, please, Mommy. Come play with me now. It is time to be happy!" The little girl smiled so brightly, so purely, that Danielle's heart broke then, in front of them all. She could not do this for herself, but she could do it for them. She could do it with His strength, because her power was not enough. She had tried to conquer this disease of her mind on her own, and it had consumed her.

Slowly, Danielle kissed her daughter with promises to meet her in a moment. She then began to pick up all of the pills and put them away. She looked to heaven and smiled. One day at a time, she would make it through. It would be hard, but God still had plans for her. She was needed here, and she could not leave her work undone.

Juliet noticed that the next set of images showed a slight improvement in Danielle's level of anxiety. Danielle would still look distressed, but then she would take action: she would address her worries; she would walk right up to the germs that so terrified her, and ever so slightly, she would face them. Timidly at first, she faced her fears; Juliet saw her talking to a woman in an office many times through the next set of images. Danielle's face continued to lighten as she expressed herself and became true to what she was – and what she could be.

In the final set of images, Danielle was shown in a large kitchen in a rundown neighborhood. She was shaking hands with everyone, serving plates of sandwiches and bottles of water to those in tattered clothing and dirty shoes. There was no fear on her face; in fact, her eyes shone with a radiance Juliet had never seen before. As she headed home from that dinner, Juliet could see her car driving down the highway. First, she could see Danielle in the driver's seat; she could almost hear the soothing song playing on her radio. Suddenly, a car from the oncoming traffic swerved and entered her lane. Danielle had no time to react. The screen went to a bird's eye view, and a moment later, Juliet watched as the cars collided. Then, the screen went black.

Juliet could hear cheers in the stands as the blinding light on stage moved toward Danielle.

"Well done, good and faithful servant," He said.

Danielle exhaled and stood calmly before Him as He continued.

"You went through an extraordinary trial on earth. It tested that part of every human that is the most challenging to control: the mind. You found My strength to overcome and used it to help others. Your life will always be an example of my power and strength to those that knew you, and even now that you are gone, your inspiration lives on."

They talked more, and at times His words and her replies were clear and Juliet could hear them easily. At other times, as they reviewed Danielle's life and discussed His original plan for her, the words were muffled and Juliet could not make them out.

In the end, Danielle stood completely still as He drew closer to her. He held out a crown, one of countless diamonds and a large amethyst in the middle. He placed it softly on Danielle's curls, and as it reflected His light, it shone brightly throughout the entire stadium.

"This is the crown of life, given to those who face trials and endure until the end. For you, it is much deserved."

Danielle bowed before Him. Then, as all the others had done before her, she took the crown from her head, admiring it briefly before laying it at His feet.

"All that I did, I did because of You. You were my strength, and I give You honor for it."

Then, Danielle began her way down the stage and another name was called. They were getting closer.

"Wasn't her crown beautiful?" the little voice beside Juliet asked. "Purple is my favorite color."

Juliet turned to Melanie. "I love purple too. But more than anything, I just hope I get a crown."

"I hope so too. I've noticed some people don't get crowns. They look so sad. But what I don't understand is why everyone gives their crown back," Melanie said, clearly regretting the fact that she would not get to keep the crown atop her flowing blonde curls.

"I think it's because we don't really deserve the crown; God is the one who got us here, and anything we have accomplished is actually far less than what we could have done. I also bet there is much more in store for us," Juliet said. So far, everything in heaven had exceeded her expectations, defied them even.

Melanie nodded. "I understand. I just wish we could keep those beautiful crowns," she said and giggled.

Juliet couldn't help but agree. She hoped that when it was her turn to approach God, her motives would be entirely pure and she would not hesitate when she returned the crown to Him. She wanted to make Him proud.

Another name was called. Juliet saw a man rise from his seat and begin to walk towards the stage. He carried himself with a confidence and appeared to be eager to review his life on the big screen.

Scenes flashed in front of the crowd. The man as he grew; his teenage years; college and beyond. Often, he was shown in a church, kneeling and praying or singing in front of a congregation. Later on, he began speaking and appeared to be in a leadership role.

Juliet could hear the crowd of his family and friends cheering. The man himself could not keep a smile off of his face.

But as he approached the Light and went onto the stage, a deep sadness fell over the crowd. It was as if everyone could sense that something was wrong, something was not as it should be.

They began to review the man's life, and though there were many accomplishments, it was clear that something was missing. Then, He spoke.

"James, you did well, but there was much more that could have been done. I gave you many gifts; your life was a blessed one. But you were content to do the surface things that man saw and applauded. You did just enough to make yourself happy, and then you stopped."

A scene flashed on the screen. James was in an ornate office, sitting in front of an older man with graying hair.

"It is time," the older man said and James smiled. This was it. This was his chance to finally take the reins of the pastoral leadership. This mega-church, with all of its parishioners and esteem, would soon look to him for direction and with awe and respect. He felt like the past few years as the associate pastor had gone on forever, and he knew he could do a much better job than his superior, but he had been patient. He had waited and smiled and dutifully done all that had been asked of him. He had suffered through all of that so that he could get to this moment.

"I am ready, sir."

"Good! Now, I know it might not be what you were expecting…" the older man began, and James looked up quickly. "…but a good friend of mine from a Louisiana parish is retiring. It's a small but respectable congregation. A good place for you to make your name and build your reputation."

"But I already have a reputation, sir. Here. The people here know me, and if I may say so, they love me. I thought, and there is no rush at all, that one day I would humbly step up and assist you in a transition of leadership. Again, whenever you are ready."

The old man sighed deeply.

"James, I hope I have not misled you. You have been a wonderful associate here, but one day, my son will take over. When the time is right, he will begin his ministry here at the church."

"Your son? He's only 16! He's a child! The people will never respect him."

"And I am only 54. Just how quickly did you think I was going to retire? James, I plan on preaching for as long as the good Lord is willing and my voice will allow me. I am in no rush to relinquish my role to anyone. And, to be honest with you, while I am pleased with all that you have done, you still have a long way to grow before you are ready to lead such a large congregation."

James stood then, offended to his very depth and in disbelief over the direction this conversation had taken.

"I suppose that the past few years have all been for nothing then. Pastor Robison over at the Northwest Bible Church has been trying to get me to work for him for years, but I thought for sure you had better plans for me. I guess it's time to give him a call."

"James, I understand your desire to jump into something big and great, but I wish you would consider this offer in Louisiana. I have prayed about it for some time. I didn't want to let you go either; you have so much potential. But I feel that it's where He wants you to go."

"How many are in the congregation?" James asked, before he dismissed the offer outright.

"There are about 240 right now, but it's growing. It's a great opportunity for you, son."

James shook his head. "I've already paid my dues here for so long. I've done everything you've asked me to; I've shown the servant's heart. But I've had enough. I'm ready for my time to shine; I'm ready for the spotlight – and not in front of some piddly crowd. I am ready for the big time. Guess I'll go give Robison a call. Thanks for all you've done, but I've got to make this happen…"

And those were the last words he spoke to the man who had been his mentor. He was readily accepted at the Northwest Bible Church, and he did indeed make a name for himself. He was the associate pastor within a year and was waiting to take over the leadership role at the church when a small aircraft crash on his way to start a mission in Guatemala ended his time on earth.

James was proud of all that he had done; sure, he'd never become the mega-preacher that he had hoped for, but he had gotten really close. And he had started so many missions that he had lost count. There was not a doubt in his mind that he would be praised for his efforts.

Suddenly, a collage of faces began to show on the screen and His voice filled the stadium.

"James, for all the results you thought you accomplished, there was so much more. If you had stopped all of the busywork and glory-seeking activities, these were the lives you were meant to help. And this was what I had planned for you."

Images began to play, showing James in Louisiana. He brought an excitement to the congregation that the parishioners had never experienced. The word quickly spread, and they couldn't keep visitors away. Before long, a new building was needed. And then another one. Soon, they took over a large industrial complex in the center of town, the only facility big enough to hold their massive crowd.

James stood on a large stage, and, as he had always dreamed, preached to thousands. There were multiple services and week-long events that they coordinated and hosted; his church had completely taken over and transformed the town.

The screen showed James traveling across the world, bringing immeasurable aid to the impoverished nations to which he ministered. He worked day and night with the workers already stationed there, bringing them relief as well. It showed him kneeling in prayer with crowds of men, women, and children. These were the countless lives he was supposed to save and change.

James felt his eyes filled with tears, and as the screen went black, they were streaming down his cheeks. What had he done? What had he missed?

Slowly, He approached James and wiped the tears away.

"There were many opportunities that you missed, but now you see why it should have been different. The servant's heart that you thought you understood never had a chance to develop in you. But do not worry, James. Here, you will be able to continue your work."

No other explanation was given. Juliet wondered if he would be punished here in heaven for the opportunities he had missed on earth. What would his penance be? Juliet looked around her at the sea of faces and wondered how many of them had done well and how many of them had shrunk away from their potential and sought something else instead? Had she done that with her own life?

Suddenly feeling so alone in the midst of the gigantic crowd, Juliet grabbed her viewing screen. She thought of her family and was pleasantly surprised when the screen settled in on a graduation ceremony down on earth. It didn't take her long to realize that it was Ellie's high school graduation. Juliet felt the familiar stinging in her eyes as an image of Ellie filled her screen. Her heart ached for the moments she had missed with her daughter. Ellie still had the same dark hair and green eyes, but her features had thinned and she had become a woman. Juliet could see so much of herself in Ellie, and as she touched the screen softly, she wished with all of her heart that it was her daughter's cheek instead of the cool glass. Still, she was so happy to see her daughter there and she listened closely to the program, hoping to catch a few hints about Ellie's accomplishments. But Ellie was never mentioned, and as the commencement grew to a close, it seemed as if no one even knew her name. When Ellie walked across the stage, there had only been a few claps in the crowd, and Juliet had strained to see Mark and Grace, along with two other women. She didn't want to dwell on that and instead turned her focus back to Ellie.

Ellie's eyes seemed glued to the ground, and as soon as the principal had concluded the ceremony, she made a bolt for the door. Never even checking in with her family, Ellie got into her car and slowly drove away.

Juliet could see Ellie's hands shaking as she maneuvered her small car. She could see tears dripping down her cheeks, and

Juliet tried desperately to bang on the screen to catch her attention and then to whisper through it, to tell Ellie that it was going to be okay.

Ellie drove to the Fairview Dam a little ways outside of town. It was a place that Juliet and Mark had taken the girls when they were little, and they had all been so fascinated by the roaring water at the bottom of the steep drop. Ellie walked onto it now, and as she neared the edge, Juliet could remember grabbing her hand when she was a small girl and telling her to stay back. The protective railing did not seem any higher now than it had been fifteen years earlier, and Juliet tensed as she saw Ellie wander closer and closer to it.

For a long time, Ellie just stood at the edge of the dam, watching the water, crying, and looking heavenward. Finally, she began to climb on the ledge and Juliet caught her breath. Ellie stood there for a moment and put her arms out wide, as though she was getting ready to fly. Juliet froze. She wanted to scream for help; someone had to save her. But a second later, Ellie simply climbed down and walked back to her car. Still crying, still shaking, still alone.

As Juliet stared at the scene before her, fear gripped at her heart, and she turned to Harold beside her for reassurance. But he wasn't there. As she started to search for him, it happened.

"Juliet Mathews, please come forward."

Juliet's eyes opened wide. Her breath caught in her throat, and she felt a clenching in her stomach. How had she missed Harold's story? How did time pass so quickly? How was it already her turn?

Juliet stood and was surprised to find her legs a little shaky. She looked across the crowd, and it felt as though every eye was on her. She froze for a moment, unsure if she could move forward.

And then she heard it: a quiet clapping that soon turned into a roaring cheer. She looked up and was surprised to see a large collection of people in the stands, standing and facing her. They were yelling her name and some were jumping in the air.

Juliet couldn't help but smile. Who were these people? She looked closer and soon identified her grandparents from her mom's side. They both had tears in their eyes and grinned from ear to ear. Juliet could almost feel their joy. There were a handful of aunts, uncles, and cousins she had grown up with and seen briefly at family reunions. She realized there were people there that she didn't even recognize – she didn't know them, but somehow they knew her. And they had been praying for her.

Then, Juliet saw Tammy, her best friend from college, and she felt her heart race. Tammy had passed away three years before Juliet after a brutal battle with breast cancer. Juliet remembered praying with her at the hospital, night after night, believing that God would heal her friend from this disease. Juliet knew God wanted to use Tammy as an example of the power of prayer. It had been so devastating when she had died.

For months after, Juliet hadn't been able to talk to God. Every time she knelt in prayer or closed her eyes to focus, she felt a hot anger well in her heart. She didn't understand how He could take this young, vibrant mother and wife. Tammy had just delivered her second son when they found the lump. They had aggressively treated her with chemotherapy and radiation. Juliet still remembered crying with her friend as her beautiful auburn locks had fallen out in clumps. Bit by bit, Tammy fell apart, and as much as she hated to see her friend go, Juliet had been thankful when the pain was over. Still, it was excruciating as she hugged Tammy's little boys. They wouldn't stop asking for their mommy for months.

But then, they had stopped, and it was almost just as sad to see the memories of their mom slowly slipping away.

Juliet wondered if her daughters would forget her. Would they miss her always? Juliet didn't know what to hope for; she didn't want them to be sad but she always wanted to be a part of them. As it was with much of motherhood, Juliet's emotions were conflicted. She wondered now what Tammy had learned about her family. How had they managed without her?

Juliet looked forward to learning more about how all this pain worked into His plan. She waved excitedly at Tammy and the others in her section, and then slowly began her walk to the stage. With her friends and family cheering her on, she suddenly felt like this wouldn't be so bad. They had all made it through; they were proud of her no matter what.

The steadiness returned to her legs and she moved forward confidently. Now, it was time to face the music.

This big screen version of her life was much like the flash she had experienced at her death, but this time, everything was much slower and in greater detail. She saw her life growing up, her parents, her childhood friends. She saw the tree swing in her backyard that she had spent countless hours swinging on – pushed by her dad when she was little and all by herself as she grew older. She remembered it as a place of peace and relaxation.

Juliet saw teachers and teammates and families that she had known all of her life. At one point, the movie seemed to slow down, and Juliet was taken back to a time she wished with all of her heart could be forgotten. She was almost 16, a sophomore in high school. Her life was so blessed – a starter on the basketball team, a clarinet player in the band, and a member of the student council leadership. She had more friends than she could count, and almost everyone knew her name.

At the end of the year, she was invited to a New Year's Eve party attended by many juniors and seniors, the people that she was desperate to befriend. She wanted to be one of them, cool and accepted.

She knew there was a lot of drinking at these parties, but she had never been tempted before. Tonight however, her resolve was weakened as the football captain (and quite possibly the most handsome boy on earth) offered her a beer. She took it immediately, never intending to drink it.

But as they stood there talking for minutes that became hours, he took it from her hand and opened it, toasting her with his own bottle. She hesitated for only a moment before taking a drink herself. The taste was hard and bitter, and she had to fight not to spit it out. Somehow, she managed a second drink and then a third. Soon, her mouth was numb to the taste, and her new friend was grabbing her another bottle.

They drank and talked for hours, and Juliet thought this was absolutely the best night of her life. When the sun began to rise and she realized she had to get home before her parents woke up, he offered to take her.

The thought that they were both severely inebriated did not cross her mind. She just needed to get home, fast. She laughed as they flew down the empty back roads. Juliet was from a small, rural community and no one appeared to be out and about at this early hour.

But as they rounded a corner five miles from her house, a black truck in the other lane took them by surprise. The football captain had taken the turn slow and wide, and the truck was into his front bumper before there was a chance to react.

He had died instantly; Juliet had escaped with only a broken arm and leg, which seemed so small in comparison but hampered her involvement in school activities for the rest of the year.

The driver of the other truck had also been killed, and Juliet remembered attending his funeral and seeing the tears in his wife's eyes and the sobs of his daughter and son.

The guilt she had felt at that moment ensured that she would never, ever drink again. The taste of alcohol was forever linked with death: blood, tears, and fear.

Now, in the massive stadium, Juliet scanned the crowd for those involved in the accident. When no familiar faces appeared, she made a mental note to search for them later. She wondered how that tragic event had affected them all. Where was the good in that agony?

Juliet also looked in the stands at her friends and family. Were they embarrassed? Devastated? After the accident, some of the details had been hidden from the public, and she had never received the backlash she felt she deserved. Now, the family that stared back at her still looked on with love and excitement. A few of them even waved.

Juliet turned back to the screen, which had now reached her college years. She had worked so hard during her four and a half years at the university. Though she was a quick learner, tests had always been a challenge for her and didn't reflect her true knowledge. The movie came to a point in her junior year when she had experienced a particularly difficult fall semester.

During the two weeks before finals, she was writing three papers while trying to finish two group projects and study for four final exams – all while working part-time at the local pool hall to try and help pay for books and tuition.

She had never felt so overwhelmed in her life. This was the first time she really didn't think she could get everything done. She felt like such a failure, and she was overwhelmed with dread in her heart when she thought about telling her mom that she had flunked her courses. They couldn't afford for her to re-take a year of classes, and she hated to let her mom down after all she had been through. She didn't need anything else to worry about.

Juliet was forced to start working at the pool hall after her dad passed away. He'd left almost everything to his new wife and not enough to her to help cover her college costs. Even in his death, he had hurt her and made her life harder. If only he had thought of someone besides himself.

In the pool hall one evening, her answer appeared. She was waiting on a group of students in the back corner of the establishment. They were laughing and drinking, annoying Juliet immensely as she desperately wanted to just let go herself for one night and relax. She resentfully served them their drinks and snacks for hours and, as they were getting ready to leave, she happened to overhear part of their conversation.

"Here is my fifty." Juliet looked up to see a girl handing one of the guys a wad of cash. Several others followed suit.

"When do we get the tests? I want to make sure I have time to memorize the answers."

The guy with all the money looked confident as he shoved the bills into his pocket.

"No worries. The tests will be ready tomorrow. Just let me know what classes you need, and you will have them in plenty of time."

Juliet couldn't believe it. This was her answer. She had tried to do too much, and this was her way out.

She approached the group slowly. The guy with all the money saw her coming and smiled. He must have been able to read the hopelessness in her eyes. Before they left, Juliet had given him $150 of her hard-earned money in exchange for a phone number and a meeting place that would solve all of her problems.

In the end, she had passed the tests as promised, and the screen soon showed her walking across the college stage and accepting her diploma. But her success and the pride that came with that had been tempered. Inside, she always felt like she had received something she didn't deserve. Her confidence in herself had been damaged, and she regretted that choice for the rest of her life.

Now the screen was flying through the rest of her college years and into her marriage. It showed her interacting with Mark, some days with love and some days with anger. She saw some of the fights they had gone through, and she instantly wished she could take back the hateful words she had yelled at him. Why did she have to be so sensitive? Why did she demand so much of him? He was, of course, only human.

She saw herself with her girls, holding them close, rocking them to sleep, changing diaper after diaper, cleaning up mess after mess. For a few years there, she felt as though she had lived in the laundry room. It was reassuring then to see that all of her effort had not gone unnoticed, to know that what had seemed to be unseen had actually been appreciated.

Being a mom had been no picnic. There had been so many days when she wanted to scream and run out the door. All the fighting, all the whining, all of the endless demands. It seemed like she never had a moment to herself. Mark tried to help, but in the end, it all came back to her. And sometimes that had been overwhelming.

But in some of the last scenes with her daughters and her husband, she could feel their love. She knew that all of her tireless days and nights had not been in vain. She had shown them the unconditional love and forgiveness that mirrored the One who stood before her now.

Her life-ending car crash was a blur, and then the screen went black. Juliet then realized that she had reached the stage. She lifted her foot to take the first step and stopped. Before her, the light shone brilliantly. From her seat in the crowd, she hadn't been able to see much more than glaring brightness and a blur of movement, but now that she was so close, she could see clearly.

In the midst of the light was a man-like figure. He was tall with dark hair and dark eyes. His form was one of strength and power, and Juliet instantly felt humbled and weak before Him. As she looked closer, she realized that His eyes were watching hers.

Instantly, she felt a jolt – a mixture of excitement, fear, and disbelief. God's eyes were locked on hers. The Creator of all things, the Ruler of the universe, was looking directly at her. She wondered then how often He had been looking directly at her during her life on earth, and the thought made her both proud and sad. The disappointment He would feel every day as He watched over His beloved children must have been overwhelming at times.

He extended His hand toward her, and Juliet slowly took it. His grasp was strong, and as He lead her to the middle of the stage, she felt a calmness run from His hand to hers.

"Are you ready, Juliet?" He asked. His voice was both authoritative and loving, a combination she had long sought after as a mom.

"Yes, Sir," she said. And then it began.

9 / ELLIE AT TWENTY

When she found the journals, Ellie was surprised that Grace had not noticed them first. On a visit home from college, Ellie's dad suggested she go into the attic and look through some of her mom's things. Apparently, he had saved everything. With her budget at an abysmal level, Ellie was hoping to find an outfit or two that might fit and not look completely outdated.

Not that she really cared. The few friends that Ellie associated with definitely did not care about appearances. In fact, you could most likely spend an entire evening in front of them wearing nothing and they would not notice. They didn't notice much…just floated through life, waiting for the next time they could escape all the realities, the harshness, the pain.

Ellie fit in quite nicely. There were no expectations of her, just acceptance and relief if she helped them fund the next round. She worked shifts as a waitress at a diner near campus and contributed whenever she could to the group. Most of her money was consumed with tuition, books, food, room and board – the bare necessities. Her father helped as much as he could, but with both Grace and Laynie attending college as well, funds were scarce. And Ellie knew she took a lower priority.

As she started to dig through her mom's old belongings, dust shot into the air, and then drifted down, caught in slow motion by the sunlight streaming in through the attic's single window. Ellie choked back a cough and blew away as much dust as she could. First, she found the outfits. Skirts, blouses, pinstriped slacks...all professional pieces that she had no need of right now. There were some floral dresses that Ellie had vague memories of her mother wearing as they all went to church together. Then, the jackpot: a box full of relaxed pants and T-shirts, as well as sweatshirts and jackets for the upcoming fall.

Ellie was stuffing it all into a large trash bag for transportation home when she noticed the other boxes. The first one contained piles and piles of pictures, yellowed and faded with age. They seemed to cover decades, and Ellie remembered some of the pictures from when she was little. It still hurt to look at them, with her mom smiling so brightly. In fact, the whole family smiled except for Ellie. As she thumbed through image after image, she realized that there was never one of her laughing or grinning. She always had the same expression – not really mad, not really happy. Just there. Waiting for the bad thing to happen.

She had that same expression in photos today. Still, she wasn't really mad or sad, just waiting. But this time, she wasn't really sure what she was waiting for.

The next box was full of books: romance novels, westerns, an old Bible. Ellie definitely did not share her mother's taste in reading. She read only what she had to, and her college texts consumed all of her time at present. She'd never been much into reading fiction; the endings were always happy, and to Ellie, that wasn't real. In real life, things didn't always turn out the way they should.

The final box held the journals. There were at least fifteen or twenty of them, each one dated with a year. The first one started back in 1968. Ellie did the math and realized that her mother must have been around 15 at the time. She opened the hot pink and purple book and began to read.

It feels like my life is over. I don't understand how it happened so fast. One minute, all I worried about was practicing my clarinet or making sure I could make ten free throws in a row. Now, I have to figure out what I should wear to a funeral…for the boy I killed.

Ellie's eyes grew wide. What was this? Her parents had never mentioned a murder? She read on, deciphering the teenage scribbling to determine that the incident really involved a horrible car accident and that her mother wasn't directly at fault.

But her guilt must have been unbearable. Ellie read the next few pages to see that her mother had since given up alcohol. When she thought about it, she realized that she could never remember her mom taking a drink, even a sip of wine on holidays. But her memories had long since become hazy, so much so that she didn't trust them anymore.

Ellie clearly had not waited until the legal age limit to begin indulging in adult beverages. As soon as she discovered the numbing properties of alcohol, she was drawn to it. It dulled her aches and masked over her fears. It was the perfect ending (or beginning) to most days. She always drank responsibly and never got behind the wheel if she was drunk. In fact, she tried to avoid getting behind the wheel at all costs.

Now, her group of friends had taken it beyond drinking and were experimenting with a variety of mindless and intoxicating substances. Ellie was tempted to join them. When she wasn't studying or in class, she wanted to be free of herself and her thoughts, and this seemed like the easiest way to accomplish that goal.

Ellie read until the middle of 1972, when her dad called her down for dinner. She grabbed the bag of clothes and the box of journals and headed to the table. After a filling meal of hamburgers and corn on the cob, she pecked her dad on the cheek and headed back to campus. She was surprisingly anxious to continue reading. Maybe her mom had a message for her somewhere in there.

***

Ben didn't want to wake up that morning. When his eyes first flickered open, he shut them again tightly, trying to block out the bright light that announced the new day. There was so much to dread in the next eight hours…a massive report worth half his grade due at noon, an unbelievably comprehensive chemistry exam at one, and (his least favorite of all) an oral report to be delivered in front of two hundred of his nearest and dearest classmates at three that afternoon. The end of the semester brought so much pain, and he still had two more years to go.

Though he'd heard that most colleges got more intense as the years went by, he felt this year was taking it to a new level. There was no humanly way possible he could get everything done that he needed to.

Get up, get moving. Time to face the day. There it was again, that voice inside of him that begged to be ignored. Ben closed his eyes. No need to get up. No reason to try. There was no way he could do it.

Come on, you can do this. You are ready. Ben forced his eyes open and glared heavenward. Somehow, he'd always made it through before, but today…he just didn't know. He shut his eyes once more and rolled over in the bed. Maybe one more hour of sleep would help. Maybe it would give him the energy he needed to survive the day. Or maybe he would somehow keep sleeping and the day would fade away, and he would deal with the rest later.

Ben, you don't mean that. You will be fine. Now, get up and get your day started.

Ben groaned and threw back the sheets. He was tired of arguing with himself. He always lost those battles anyway; he might as well give up now.

As if on cue, the smell of fresh coffee wafted slowly and enticingly through his room. His roommate must have left their door open again. He had a habit of heading out early in the morning for his regular jog and leaving their front door cracked so he didn't need to carry his key. So thoughtful.

For once though, Ben was thankful for his roommate's carelessness. That pull of a freshly brewed cup was the only thing that might get him out the door that morning. That jolt of energy – he needed it bad.

He had hated coffee until he got to college. Instead of turning to other stimulants to help him through the night, he chose the classic solution: a burst of caffeine that never let him down.

That decision was typical of the choices he had made throughout his young life. He was all for having a good time, but had no desire to lose control or make a fool of himself. His parents had worked hard and saved every month to send him to college, and though this was not the most elite of universities, it was still costly and he wanted to make them proud.

He remembered several times in high school when his friends had wanted to get lost somewhere and get drunk, and he had gone along with them. He hadn't fought or argued or criticized their choices, but he had no intention of joining in their revelry. Instead, it played out the same way every time; he would be the designated driver. It was a role he seemed to fill for several of his friends; he was the one who chose to stay on the straight and narrow and kept watch for any trouble that may be on the horizon. And he didn't mind that at all. It wasn't like he didn't mess up or do stupid things occasionally, but on most occasions, he just had no desire to get crazy. This had been a source of frustration for several of the girls he had dated in college, but that didn't bother him. He knew the right girl would come along at the right time. He was in no rush.

Still not fully awake but desperately in need of his coffee fix, Ben grabbed a T-shirt from the pile on the floor and staggered down the hall to the common area shared by the residents on that floor. He made eye contact with no one; instead, he made a beeline straight for the steaming pot in the corner.

The warm liquid coated his throat. He muttered a barely audible "ahhh" before he noticed a pair of eyes staring at him.

"Help yourself," a slightly annoyed feminine voice said, and Ben looked up to see a girl with jet black hair sitting on the main couch. She was sipping her own cup of the magic brew and was surrounded by a collection of multi-colored books that seemed to envelope her.

"Sorry, it was a long night," he paused and took a deep breath. "Going to be a long day."

Ellie looked up at him again and his eyes locked with hers. She wanted to turn away, but all of a sudden, she couldn't seem to move. It felt as though he could see right thought her, and for a moment, she couldn't speak. She had never seen eyes so blue.

"No, it's not a problem," she muttered, turning back to her journals. Why did his stare seem so piercing? "I'm in a bad mood; just ignore me."

He nodded to her and then refilled his cup slowly.

Ellie began to read again from the mountain of journals that she couldn't seem to put down. She had made it to 1978, the year her parents met. Her mom was obviously smitten with this new love in her life.

Something I have learned…When you find love, you will know it. Something inside you will pause; something will make you look back and wonder. It may not happen right away, but the seed will be planted, and one day, a flower of love and light and hope will grow. You will see your future and everything will seem possible.

Ellie set the book down, and Ben met her eyes once more. He offered her a slight smile as he took his cup and turned to leave. She looked away quickly, but as he headed back to his room, Ellie found herself glancing up to watch him go.

10 / THE WHYS

The giant screen began to replay Juliet's life, this time in slow detail. Somehow, she was able to remember each moment, each choice, each decision with an amazing clarity. Not only that, but she relived the emotions she had felt during each scene.

They began to go through each moment together. He would pause the screen to ask her why she had chosen to react in a certain way. She would respond to Him with her honest recollection, no matter if it was something she was proud of or something she had done wrong.

In the instances where her decisions had been poor, he would replay the scene – this time in such a way that Juliet saw what should have happened and what impact she could have made. These moments were heartbreaking as Juliet realized all the possibilities she had squandered each and every day.

During high school, they arrived at her junior year. Basketball season was in full swing, and Juliet was starting on the Varsity. This was her dream come true. She practiced hard and played hard and enjoyed giving her all to this sport she adored.

In the middle of the season, her team was facing one of its biggest competitors. It wasn't a team from their district but one that they played every year and loathed, like all good rivals. In the third quarter, Juliet was passing a ball to their point guard when the girl suddenly fell down on the court. She was writhing in pain, grasping at her right knee, tears pouring down her face. They had all seen this injury before: a blown out knee. It was a devastating and cruel ailment that seemed to come out of nowhere and would likely mean the end of the season for the player.

The point guard was taken off on a stretcher to the trainer's office, and the game continued. Juliet's team ended up winning, but instead of celebrating with her friends after the victory, she went to find her injured teammate.

That didn't take long. The player, with tears still streaming down her face, was waiting in the trainer's office. A doctor had come to take a closer look, and they would soon be transporting her to the hospital for further analysis. Juliet could see the fear and disbelief on the player's face. This was everyone's worst nightmare, especially for the talented group on Juliet's team; they all had higher aspirations to continue playing at the collegiate level, and none seemed more likely to move on than their point guard.

Juliet stayed with the girl for the rest of the night, even going to the hospital with her. Though her teammate never said thank you, Juliet often found her hand being clenched tightly as more tears flowed.

The season continued and Juliet's team was destined for the playoffs. This was her big chance to perform in front of the few scouts that had started to take notice of women's basketball and make her name known on a national level.

As the weeks went by, everyone forgot their injured teammate. At first, they had all visited her often, even bringing balloons and a stuffed tiger, which resembled their mascot. But not long after, the season took a hold of them, along with homework and dating and all of the seemingly important things on a teenager's mind.

Right before the playoffs, Juliet remembered her friend. She realized it had been weeks since she'd seen her. She didn't come to the games anymore; apparently watching everyone else compete was just too much. Juliet knew she had been doing lots of physical therapy, but when she went to the trainer's office to check on her, she wasn't there. For the rest of the day, Juliet searched for the girl. Finally, after practice, she got her address from the coach and drove over to her home.

As she drove, Juliet noticed that the neighborhood around her was deteriorating. Juliet's family was far from rich, but they had food on the table every night and closets full of clothes. Juliet even had her own vehicle to drive, though it was a used pick-up truck, nearly on its last leg.

When Juliet found the house she was looking for, she hesitantly walked up the steps. Lightly, she knocked on the door. As she waited, she noticed the peeling paint and disheveled front porch. Parts of the fence were leaning and the whole thing looked as though it might fall down at any moment.

When no one answered, Juliet tapped softly once again. Part of her was really hoping no one would answer. A moment later, the door opened slightly.

"Who is it?" came the crackly voice from inside.

"Uh…I'm Juliet, a teammate of Jana's. Is she home?"

The door opened a little more and an elderly woman with dark black eyes and white hair stared back at her.

"Jana is in her room. Please, come in."

Juliet followed the old woman to the back of the house, trying not to notice the piles of laundry and dishes as she went.

The woman opened the back bedroom door and ushered Juliet inside.

"Go on in. Maybe you can help."

Juliet entered, and for a moment, she could not see in the dimly lit room.

"Jana?"

Suddenly there was movement from the direction of the bed.

"Juliet! What are you doing here? How did you find me?"

As her eyes adjusted to the darkness, Juliet sat on the bed beside her teammate. Despite the girl's protest, she would not leave. She learned that Jana had stopped going to physical therapy and stopped going to school completely on most days.

"You can't give up, Jana. We need you. You were our star player."

Jana looked at her slowly, and Juliet saw the tears slowly start to trickle down her friend's cheeks.

"I *was* your star player. You don't need me anymore. Look how far you've made it without me. Basketball was my only hope to get out of this dump. And now, it's gone. The doctor says I might not be able to play next season, even if I do all of my therapy. What's the point then? I've been working so hard for nothing. And everyone has forgotten me."

Juliet didn't know if she should acknowledge the truth in her friend's statement. Instead, she offered to help. She convinced Jana to return to school and to continue therapy with a promise that she would be right there by her side.

"We still have our senior year to look forward to. And I want you leading our team to the state championship," she said, hoping Jana couldn't hear the hint of doubt in her words.

Jana smiled then, and it was like a ray of sunshine lighting up that dim, depressing room. Even if Juliet wasn't completely sure of the outcome, her little offer of hope was all Jana needed.

They agreed on a deal and stuck with it, though it meant Juliet had to stay long hours after school, first for her own practice and then for Jana's physical therapy. Soon, other girls on the team noticed what was going on and offered to help out. Jana was a part of the team once again.

The next scene on the big screen showed a game during their senior year of high school. Jana ran out on the court, and though she could not play for most of the year, she was able to contribute to their championship season.

Juliet smiled at the memory, and looked up at Him.

"You showed love to that girl, Juliet, and that is the greatest gift you could give. When everyone else had forgotten or was too busy with *important* things, you did the most important thing of all. You reached out to her. You saved her, Juliet.

Without basketball and without the support of your team, Jana was quickly heading down a bad path. Your actions were exactly as I had planned."

As He spoke, Juliet noticed that a pile had started to grow beside her. This pile was comprised of a strange group of materials: she saw hay and straw amidst silver and gold. Now, a few precious stones of various colors appeared. Before she had a chance to wonder more about the interesting mass, the screen began to show more images.

Juliet was in her high school office where she worked as an assistant during third period her senior year. Only students with good grades and recommendations from their teachers were allowed to work in the office, so Juliet took great pride in being one of the chosen few.

It was right after spring break when Taylor Allen arrived at their school. Juliet remembered the day the thin, blonde girl showed up as a transfer student. Instantly, a buzz started about her; she was a basketball player, she was one of the smartest students from her old school, she had been on the homecoming court.

Juliet couldn't deny her beauty; boys walked into walls watching her during the first few weeks after she arrived. Especially one boy: Jeffrey Anderson – the boy Juliet had been working up the nerve to talk to all year long. They had a few classes together; he had come to some of her games. He was really smart and handsome but painfully shy, and Juliet hadn't wanted to push him. Most of the girls at the school knew about her crush and respected Jeffrey as "taken", but Taylor didn't know.

The day she saw them talking by the row of lockers on the south lawn, her heart stopped. Jeffrey was smiling, laughing even as Taylor reached out to touch his arm.

Hot anger rushed within Juliet and she stormed to the office, determined to fight for this boy.

As she headed into the school office, her assignment that day proved fortuitous. She was to make copies of certain forms from a list of students applying to local colleges. This meant she would have access to all of the students' files. She instantly decided to take a closer look at Miss Taylor Allen. She knew for sure this princess wasn't all she was cracked up to be.

She did her work for a few moments until the filing room cleared and she was left alone with a cabinet full of secrets. Quickly, she pulled the file and began to read.

All the good stuff was there: the perfect grades, the athletic report, the teacher recommendations. But in the back, she found what she had been looking for.

As a freshman at her old school, Taylor had been caught stealing another student's wallet from her purse. The incident had been handled at the school and no formal charges had been filed, but a note had been made. And Juliet had her plan.

A few days later, at lunch, the opportunity presented itself. A group of her friends were talking at a back table, and Taylor and Jeffrey were sitting a few seats down, close enough for Juliet's plan to work.

"My purse!" Juliet said suddenly and jumped up. She looked around her seat and tried to look very concerned.

Her friends stopped talking and started looking around.

"Here it is!" a girl shouted, pulling the bag from the end of the table where Juliet had stuffed it.

"Oh good," Juliet smiled, trying to show tremendous relief as her friend tossed it to her. She glanced over at Taylor.

"I was worried there for a second," she said, loudly enough so that everyone at their table could hear. "I heard about the *incident*, Taylor."

Taylor stopped talking and the beautiful grin faded from her face. All eyes were on her and Juliet could see her cheeks flushing red.

"Wh-what are you talking about?" Taylor asked and Juliet almost wished she had just run off. Did she really want to take this all the way? But she saw Jeffrey's hand touching Taylor's and decided it was worth it. This was the man she was probably going to marry.

"Oh, I meant at your old school. You probably don't want to talk about it here, and I'm sure you don't steal anymore, but I was just worried for a second."

Taylor's face drooped even more then, and the whispering started all around her. She looked over at Jeffrey who was looking at the floor, unsure of how to respond.

She slowly took her lunch and walked towards the door. A moment later, conversations started back up around the lunch room. There were a few "can you believe that?" comments at their table before previous topics were resumed.

Juliet looked at Jeffrey who was still staring at the floor. She wanted to go to him then, to talk to him and begin where they had left off, but she thought she might give him some time to digest what he had heard.

The weeks went by and Juliet's attempts at talking with Jeffrey never quite went anywhere. She noticed that he never really talked to Taylor again (not many people did), but he didn't seem interested in her anymore either.

For some reason, the passionate love that she had felt towards him faded as well. She felt guilty every time she looked at him and found herself seeking him out less and less.

She did make a point to reach out to Taylor. The blonde haired girl was understandably hesitant when Juliet approached her at lunch one day.

"I just wanted to say I'm sorry, Taylor, for saying the things that I did. That was wrong of me, and you have every right to hate me."

Taylor looked up at her. "Good, because I do. But don't worry, I'm done with this place. I've already been accepted at Wakeland University, and I am just counting the seconds until I can get out of here. Thanks to you, I have nothing to miss."

Juliet stood beside her for a few minutes, really unsure of what to say next. She had ruined someone's senior year and there was nothing she could do about it.

She tried for a few weeks to talk to Taylor, but all of her attempts were rebuffed, and by the time they all graduated in May, she had all but forgotten the incident.

On the big screen, the events that Juliet had just watched seemed even worse than when she had lived them on earth. How could she have done something so awful? All for a boy who she didn't really even know? It was hard to believe she had made such a horrible decision, and she was scared now to face His stare.

But as she looked up at Him, she only saw love.

"Juliet, you see now how poor those choices you made were. You asked for forgiveness, and it was given to you, but the actions that you took affected the plan that I had. Please watch."

She turned back to the screen, back to her high school. She saw Taylor and Jeffrey together, holding hands. She saw them on their first date, on a trip to the movie, on a day at the beach. They were happy, laughing, completely in love.

She saw them then at a church, Jeffrey's church. Taylor was visiting, smiling as she was accepted and greeted by the members.

Time went by and there was a wedding, children, happiness and joy.

Juliet watched, horrified. She had ruined all of that? Her actions had taken all of that out of play?

"Oh, no, Juliet. It still happened," He said, seeing the fear and overwhelming guilt on her face. "Just not in the way that I had planned. Taylor went through many trials in college; she had to navigate many temptations and evils that I had hoped she would avoid. But, in the end, Jeffrey found her again, with maybe a little help from some of us up above," He said and smiled.

Before she had time to dwell on what He had told her, more images began to play. Juliet saw herself at the hospital. Though she loved her job as a nurse, day after day she got stuck with the responsibilities everyone else avoided: cleaning out bedpans, dealing with patients who returned week after week with no known ailments, responding quickly to a doctor's urgent request. She saw image after image of herself bathing patients, giving them the medications they didn't want to take, gently inserting IVs into arms that were shaking with fear.

Juliet also saw herself in the car, struggling with directions, as she headed to her home health visits. In addition to her regular hours at the hospital, she also took on assignments after hours and on the weekends. In these cases, she would travel to the homes of those who needed assistance and chose to receive their care outside of the hospital. In many cases, the homes she visited were in areas she would have avoided any other day.

Once the images of her nursing days finished, He smiled broadly at her.

"You chose well with your career. There were many positions you could have selected, but being a nurse perfectly utilized the gifts I gave you of serving, healing, and compassion. There were so many times when you gave of yourself when you had nothing left to give. When you were tired and didn't want to work the nightshift that nobody else wanted, still you went in, because you thought of those that needed you. When the patients you risked your safety for grumbled and criticized your every move, still you continued your home health visits. Through the trials and danger, you stood strong. And for that, you will receive your reward."

Juliet noticed the pile beside her filling with beautiful gems of every color and size. They sparkled and reflected brilliantly from His light.

And then they moved on.

Face after face appeared on the screen. These were not friends or family members; in fact, these were people she must have seen only once in her life because her extra clear memory could barely recall them at all. Soon, she noticed a pattern. Typically they were older men with graying hair and straggling beards. They wore tattered clothing and always appeared outside. These were the people she had seen by the side of the road. Many of them she had only glanced at for a second. Most of them she had never thought of again. The stream of faces continued until the scene shifted to the inside of Juliet's car.

"Mom," a very young Grace began. "Why is that man holding a sign? What does it mean?"

Juliet looked back at her daughter, at first not even sure what the little girl was referring to. Then, she noticed the homeless man standing near their car. She immediately checked to make sure their doors were locked before turning to address Grace.

"That poor man doesn't have a home. He doesn't have any food to eat or water to drink, and he is asking for someone to help him."

"Then, why don't you?" Grace asked. The answer seemed so clear to the little girl, but Juliet couldn't help but think of what might happen if she rolled down her window and let the man approach. She had heard horror stories of people being robbed, thrown from their cars. She had two little girls to think about; though the odds of anything bad happening were slim, she couldn't risk it. She *wouldn't* risk it.

"Mom?" Grace asked. She was waiting for an answer.

"I will think of a way to help him," Juliet said as the light turned green and she sped away from her nagging conscience.

It wasn't until a month later that Juliet remembered her promise. She was in the car alone, on her way to work, and noticed another homeless person at a red light. This was an older woman, pulling a large sack stuffed with clothes, papers, food. Probably all of her worldly possessions, Juliet thought guiltily as she glanced down at her own nice purse and clothes. They were far from rich but they had everything they could ever need. Some people didn't have anything at all.

That was the day Juliet started a family tradition. Thanksgiving was fast approaching and she heard an announcement at church about an opportunity to serve at a soup kitchen for the holiday. She never would have considered it; they always went to Mark's mom's home and met with his extended family, enjoying an amazing spread of homemade food that left her stomach bulging for weeks.

She knew the holiday was important to Mark, but that night she approached him about serving at the soup kitchen together as a family before heading out to his mom's. They might miss a few football games and the beginning of dinner, but she felt it was worth it. He agreed.

As they served turkey and dressing, mashed potatoes, and a roll to the hundreds that gathered at the soup kitchen that morning, Juliet turned to Grace. The little girl stood beside her, excited to be responsible for the mashed potato portion of the meal.

"Grace, I want to thank you for helping everyone today," she began.

"Sure, Mom. This is awesome!" Juliet smiled; she knew Grace's attitude might not be the same a few years from now.

"I'm glad you are enjoying it. It is important that we help others. Remember that day in the car when you asked me why I didn't help that man?"

Grace nodded but Juliet wasn't sure if she did.

"Yes, that old man with the sign. I prayed for him that night," she said, surprising her mother.

"Yes, that's the one. Well, now we are helping people like him. Sometimes, you have to find a way to help that makes sense for everyone."

Grace nodded again and turned back to her potato serving.

Juliet hoped her words sunk in; she hoped she was doing the right thing. She said a silent prayer for direction and turned back to her duties at hand.

Suddenly, the screen showed a flash of images, year after year at the soup kitchen. Even though Juliet was no longer in the picture, she saw her girls (aging in every image) returning to the soup kitchen. It was a tradition they had continued even after she was gone.

He touched her hand. "Though you did not help at every opportunity that was presented, you found a way to help that also touched your family."

Juliet noticed an increase in gold in the pile beside her.

Different images appeared on the screen then, from different points in her life. Juliet saw herself as a young child, kneeling by her bed. She saw herself as a teenager, studying the

Bible at the kitchen table as she wolfed down breakfast. She saw herself as a woman, glancing heavenward for a few moments before she dashed out the door. Then, she saw herself as a mom, sometimes kneeling with her children beside their bed for nighttime prayers, and oftentimes falling asleep on the couch before she'd had a chance to offer up words of her own.

He looked at her and took her hand.

"There were many years when you let our time together fade. Everything seemed to take precedence – your children, your husband, your job. Even your volunteering time at the church and in the community grew to consume you. There were years that you were so busy, you barely had time to breathe. As important as all of those things were, My deepest hope was that you would have chosen to take more time to pause and embrace not only all that you had, but delight in our relationship as well. The more that you and I worked through those things together, the more that they fell into place, in the time and manner that they should."

Then, they were finished. As she explained all of her motives and saw all as it should have been, it became clear to her. The selfishness, the pride, the jealousy…it was all so empty and pointless. And as she bowed before Him, all that was not pure within her left, and all that remained was His love.

Before her lay the culmination of her life, displayed as a pile of straw, hay, and precious metals. Instantly, it all went up in a flame. It burned with a white hot heat and in only a moment, the straw and hay that represented those things in her life that had been frivolous and petty disappeared, and all that was left was a brilliant blue sapphire, nestled in the center of a crown of silver and gold. He took the crown and held it in His hands before offering it to her with a smile.

"This is the crown of righteousness, Juliet. You were faithful to make the most of the opportunities and gifts I gave you. Please, accept your reward."

She took the crown then and admired it for but a second before laying it at His feet. The desire to cling to the precious jewelry had left her, and she only wanted to act in such a way that would please Him.

As she rose to her feet, He touched her hand.

"Well done," He said and her heart felt the warmth of His praise. She basked in it and then began down the stage steps.

In the distance, she could see a group of familiar faces waiting for her. Would her dad be among them? She could feel her heart racing and she paused. But there was no time to wait; already, another name was being called and another life was beginning to play before the crowd.

11 / ELLIE AT TWENTY-FIVE

The knock at the door was soft and tentative, but it startled Ellie. She dropped the lipstick she was holding, and as she reached to pick it up and quickly finished applying it, she realized her hands were shaking.

Were they really doing this? Was this the biggest mistake of her life or the best decision ever?

She honestly wasn't sure, but as she thought of Ben waiting outside the door, she didn't care.

She glanced at herself in the mirror one last time before heading out, somewhat pleased with what she saw. A girl should look pretty on her wedding day.

***

The small wedding chapel looked empty and Ellie was relieved as they walked towards it. She kept waiting for Ben to stop and say he'd changed his mind or for some total stranger to walk up and try to discourage them.

But as they walked among the drunken revelers on the Strip in Las Vegas, they didn't seem to stand out at all. It was as if this huge thing they were about to do that would change their whole lives forever was just between them. And maybe that was the point.

Neon lights flashed all around them and slot machines jingled in the distance as they walked up to the building that would legally make them husband and wife.

It wasn't the most romantic setting that Ellie could picture, but it would do. As long as she was marrying Ben, she was more than happy.

As if reading her thoughts, Ben squeezed her hand.

She looked up at him, and as always, those bright blue eyes caught her breath. She looked forward to gazing into them every morning and every evening and all that was in between for the rest of her life.

"Are you sure this is what you want to do?" she asked him for what may have been the fiftieth time that day.

"Of course. I've never been surer of anything in my life. Are *you* sure you want to marry a fireman?"

Ellie held his hand tighter. His risky job was a cause for worry, but she trusted him to stay safe. Somehow, Ben was never in doubt of anything. Since that day they'd met in college almost five years ago, he had been virtually the same person. Never swayed by fraternity foolishness or collegiate explorations into darker things. Never wildly out of control or cruel to anyone. Just solid and kind and always there for her.

"At least you have a job," she said quietly and he stopped her before she could say more.

"You don't just have a job – you have two jobs! And even though you may not waitress or sell children's shoes for the rest of your life, it doesn't matter to me one bit if you did. You'll figure out what you want to do, and I'm here to help you get there."

He always made statements like that, and not only did he say them, but he stood behind them as well. He was always there to help her face the future…and the past. He knew a little of the mistakes she had made but really didn't care to hear the details, unless she was ready to share.

"I love you for who you are, not for what you've done," he always said. It made her feel safe and confident in him, and in herself. For the first time, she was allowing herself to be happy. And that scared her.

"Do you want to call your dad?" he asked her.

She thought for a moment, slowing her steps as she tried to decide the right thing to do.

They hadn't talked much since she'd graduated from college. She knew her dad was proud of her for making it through school and conquering some of the demons she encountered there, but it seemed to make him sad to be around her. It was as if she was always a reminder of what had been and what might have been.

He seemed happy enough with his new wife, and when they got together for the holidays, everyone was smiling. There was never any tension or fighting. But inside, something was missing. For all of them. And Ellie didn't know what it was, but she knew she didn't like the empty feeling she felt there.

"I think I'll call him after," she said. "In case he might try and talk me out of it."

"Do you think you could really be persuaded to leave me at that pastel blue altar, all alone with Elvis and that diva on the piano?"

She laughed and pulled him toward the chapel. She didn't want him to look too closely at her face; he might see her fears. She didn't want him to know that she had any doubts, but inside she felt something…an anxiety that wouldn't go away. She wanted to be strong for him, as he had always been for her, and she knew without a doubt she wanted to be with Ben. But this was such a big step. And who was she to think she deserved happily ever after?

***

Johnny "Elvis" Warren was adjusting his hairpiece. It was jet black and full of gel. He flashed his snarling smile in the mirror and liked what he saw. He definitely hadn't lost his touch. Though he only fulfilled these gigs when absolutely necessary, he had to admit that he enjoyed them. There was so much life in Las Vegas – pulsating, intense, over-the-top life. It was so close to life the way it was supposed to be lived. Sadly, much of the conduct here wasn't focused in the right direction and didn't reflect the purity and simplicity of real joy. But there was so much potential, and he relished the chance to try and find the positive in it. To make a few good things out of all of the bad.

Today, he had one mission, and he thought it might be a tough one…someone so close to her happiness who would do everything in her power to stop herself from truly experiencing it. And he was there to gently guide her in the right direction.

When he saw the girl in the simple white dress fleeing for the chapel exit, he knew it was time to make it happen.

***

Ben and Ellie had been standing in the lobby waiting for forty-five minutes. Though the chapel had looked empty from the outside, it turned out that dozens of couples suddenly felt the urge to solidify their relationship that night. As Ellie surveyed the group around her, swirls of doubt grew in her mind.

Most of the other couples in the chapel seemed to be severely inebriated or at least did not have a good enough grasp of their senses to be making this type of decision. Though she hadn't had anything to drink, she wondered if she was as lost as any of them. Was that what she was doing? Making a rash and stupid choice that would ruin her life? Or ruin Ben's?

A middle-aged woman in a tight leather mini-skirt hopped on the lap of her soon-to-be husband. She ran her long, red fingernails through his greasy gray hair.

"Third time's a charm!" she laughed and kissed him hard.

The old man laughed and squeezed her back. Ellie felt sick to her stomach.

To her left, she noticed another couple waiting for their turn at eternal bliss. They looked anything but happy. The girl had a hand on her stomach, rubbing it softly with a sad look in her eyes. The guy was standing as far away from her as he possibly could while still being "with" her and staring holes in the door. She could tell he wanted to be anywhere but there. She could sense his feeling of entrapment and looked up at Ben. Did he feel trapped by her? Did he feel like he owed it to her to do this? Ben's sense of honor was unmistakable and she couldn't help but feel that maybe he was doing this out of pity. Did he feel honor bound because of all that they had been through together? Surely this wasn't the wedding day he would have chosen.

Ellie thought back to the day that had changed everything. They were seniors in college, about to graduate and enter the real world, and the thought had overwhelmed her. She had floated through college, just getting by in her classes, using the time as a stall tactic for really figuring out what she wanted to do with her life. She had no clue. There had been no purpose for so long, just the conflict of a girl who was ready to die but terrified to do so.

She and Ben had been on three dates by then. They had taken their courtship very slow, and Ellie was thankful for his patience. After she met him in the common room that first morning, he had started appearing there more and more often. She was an early riser as well as a night owl, which meant she usually got very little sleep. When she sipped that first cup of coffee each morning, she slowly eased into the day, both sad and thankful for another one. When Ben started intruding on her ritual, she had been only slightly annoyed. And that told her something. She knew immediately that this guy had a strange effect on her; for the first time she remembered, she actually looked forward to seeing someone.

Ben was kind and thoughtful with her, always asking about her day, never prying or talking too much about himself. Before she knew it, Ellie found herself accepting his invitation to dinner. That first date had been so wonderful, so perfect, that Ellie vowed then and there never to see him again. It had taken him another year to convince her to give it another chance.

The morning before their graduation, Ellie had risen early as usual. Instead of heading to the common area to meet with Ben, she walked out onto her balcony. A group of students and their families were already celebrating down below, and a few of them were holding balloons. Ellie heard the group laugh as some of the balloons were released into the air. Ellie watched them drift higher and higher, mesmerized by their steady ascent toward the clouds. Something within her yearned to join them, and she stepped towards the edge of her balcony, shakily climbing onto the ledge. As she stood there, she felt herself reaching for the balloons. She imagined them heading heavenward, towards her mom and right then, she believed with absolute certainty that if she could just grab hold, they would take her with them. And then she wouldn't have to face any of these decisions about her future any more or feel alone even when she was surrounded by a college full of friends. She was ready to fly away.

A second later, right before she took that last step, Ben was at her side, grabbing her hand and pulling her off the ledge. As he held her and looked at her with questions in his eyes, he hadn't said a word. He had just waited until she was ready to talk, to explain, to heal.

She looked at Ben now as he sat across from her in the tacky little chapel in Las Vegas. His blue eyes met hers without wavering. Once again, he squeezed her hand and offered her a reassuring smile. That seemed to be his role in life, to comfort and encourage her. Would he grow to resent that? Did she depend on him too much? Would this marriage even work?

They were so different. They didn't talk about it much, but Ellie knew Ben had deeper feelings on the subject of God and religion. She knew he had plans for how to raise their future children and had asked her dozens of time to consider attending church with him. She had made excuses every time, and he hadn't really pressed it. She realized then that they had so many differences, so many things to discuss before they did this.

More than anything, when she became his wife, she worried that Ben would disappear. Maybe he would leave; maybe he would get hurt. Somehow, she feared that as soon as he became a permanent part of her, something would happen. And the love that she let herself feel for him would become a noose around her neck, squeezing the life from her with its pain.

Suddenly, Ellie couldn't be in that room any longer. She touched Ben's arm.

"I'm going to check my makeup," she said, and before he could tell her she looked beautiful, she was already out a side door and heading down a hallway.

She looked left and right, like a deer in the headlights unsure of which way to run. But running was definitely the plan. She had to get out of there. She would make it up to Ben later; she hoped he would forgive her, but then again, maybe he would be mad enough to realize he needed someone else. Someone normal. Someone who could smile with him and support him and fight life's battles with him. She didn't know if she could do that. There was a part of her that had already given up.

She wanted him to be with someone who deserved the greatness that he was; she didn't want his pity. She couldn't hesitate any longer; Ellie chose left and began to run. She could see the red blaring "Exit" sign at the end of the hall and had made it about two-thirds of the way there when a man smacked right into her.

And it wasn't just any man.

"Well, hello there, darlin'," came the familiar southern drawl. She tried to smile but didn't know what to make of this figure before her.

"I think I am about to marry you," he said and when her eyes widened, he clarified.

"There is a young man waitin' at the altar for a beautiful young lady. You fit that description," he said, and she realized she was somewhat soothed by his snarling Elvis smile. It made her feel like maybe she wasn't the crazy one.

'I—I left something in my car. I'll just grab it and be right back," she said. The lie came easily to her, though she didn't know if she was very convincing. She just desperately wanted to make it around Elvis and get to the exit.

"Were you looking for this?" he asked and dangled something small and shiny in front of her.

Without thinking, she reached for it. She slowly fingered the tiny bracelet, and felt stinging in her eyes when she noticed the ballet slipper.

"Where did you find this?" she whispered.

"The young man at the altar slipped it to me. He said to give it to you if I saw you in the hallway. I think it was his weddin' gift for ya."

She couldn't believe it. She had looked for this for years. The most prized possession of her childhood. How did Ben get a hold of it?

She had to ask him, but more than that, she knew then that she had to stand beside him.

For some reason, he understood her and loved her, and she knew that for the rest of their lives, he would try to make her happy. Even if that seemed like an impossible goal, she knew he would never give up.

And she loved him for it.

She took Elvis' sequined sleeve.

"Lead the way, sir," she said and took a deep breath. Somehow, they would figure it all out. She was ready to face forever with Ben.

12 / THE WAY IT WILL BE

Avia was waiting for Juliet as she walked down from the stage. With one sweep of her massive wings, the beautiful creature motioned towards the large gathering of people to her left.

"Please, take some time to visit with your loved ones. Then, I have much to discuss with you."

Juliet walked slowly towards the group. These were all of the people that she had been forced to say goodbye to on earth. For some, she hadn't even had the opportunity to give a last farewell. They had been taken from her in an instant, without warning and without a chance for preparation. As her death had been.

Juliet could hardly believe the number of people waiting for her. She approached the familiar faces she had seen cheering for her during her walk. Her grandparents and various relatives made up a majority of the group. Juliet smiled at their beaming faces.

Suddenly, Tammy came bursting through the crowd. She smothered Juliet in a hug that seemed to last and last and last. They were both laughing and crying tears of happiness when Tammy finally pulled away.

"Juliet, I am so excited to see you!"

"Me too," Juliet said as she squeezed her friend's hand. Maybe Tammy would show her how to bear this separation from her family, how to deal with the worry that wouldn't seem to let go.

"I know how sad you were when I passed from earth…how angry. I so desperately wanted to tell you that I was okay—that I was more than okay! Instantly, all of my pain was gone. My hair was back! It was the most amazing feeling to be whole again..."

Juliet was so relieved. She knew the intense suffering her friend had experienced, and though she had wanted her to stay on earth with her friends and family, she knew it was selfish to keep her in so much pain.

"I have so many things to share with you, but first, take a few minutes and say hi to everyone. Then, I will have the honor of showing you around the City."

Before Juliet could ask more, she was surrounded by her family. She hugged them all and thanked them for their prayers.

She was flooded with cousins that she could barely remember, friends from high school and college that she had long forgotten. They all took their turn to hug her and welcome her. It was inspiring to see so many people from her life here in heaven.

When her grandmother approached, she touched Juliet's cheek with her hand softly.

"Little Julie, it has been such a pleasure watching you grow. Every time you looked heavenward and pleaded for help, I was on my knees on your behalf. I have been so proud of you. The last time I saw you on earth, you were only a teenager, with so much life ahead of you. I know you have been through a lot, but you made it! Now, together we will pray for our family members who are still waiting on earth. They will need your prayers. Especially your little one."

Juliet's heart tightened when she mentioned Ellie. What had been happening on earth since she had last checked in? Had that new woman in Mark's life been a bad influence on her? Had she gone on to college? There was so much she wanted to tell her girls; there was so much she needed to teach them. A sadness crossed over her and her stomach ached as she missed them.

She looked around for her viewing screen and realized she must have left it at her seat. Would they get another?

Before she could worry about that for long, a man approached her from the back of the group. He looked just as he had the night he had left them so long ago; tall with ruffled gray hair. He faced her then, only able to muster a sheepish, unsure smile.

"Hi, Juliet. I am so happy and proud to see you here," her father said and Juliet stared at him. Would he try to hug her now? She knew she would let him; she harbored no ill-will towards this man whose decisions had once seemed so life-altering. She would let him speak his peace.

"Hello, Dad. It's been a long time. I'm glad to see you here as well."

He laughed softly then. "One might not have thought that I would be here, with the way I completely messed up the end of my life. But God's grace extends even that far, and I had sought forgiveness before that old heart of mine gave out."

"You didn't seek it from me," Juliet replied, surprised at herself and the honesty of her words.

He took her hand and looked directly into her eyes. In another world, before he had left them, those eyes had always shown her love, strength, and a steadfastness that she didn't think could ever be shaken. At that moment, she looked into them and saw only truth.

"You are right, Juliet. Perhaps I was too ashamed to face you. Even though your mother and I talked many times, and I begged for her forgiveness, I never came directly to you. Did your mom ever tell you that she and I had come to a sort of truce? There was nothing I could say or do that would make up for the horrible things I had done, but I was truly sorry, and she finally understood that."

Juliet was surprised again. Her mom had never mentioned these discussions; after awhile, her father's name wasn't even mentioned in their home and Juliet was too afraid to bring it up. She didn't want to hurt her mom or cause her any more pain. She had assumed that her dad had left and never thought of them again.

When they received notice later that year after he left that her father had died of a sudden heart attack, Juliet had not felt true sadness. She was sad the way you are whenever you see an obituary for someone that you've never met, sorry that someone had suffered and passed away. But she was not sad that he was gone; he had abandoned them completely and maybe had gotten just what he deserved.

"Dad, why didn't you ever try to see me again? Why did you just disappear?" she asked him now, as they stood among the clouds and it seemed fair to ask whatever came to mind.

"I tried to write you; I tried to call. But your mom never let me talk with you. And by that time, you had changed dorms and I didn't know how to get through to you on campus. If I had known how short my time on earth was, I would have definitely made more of an effort. I just assumed that time would heal those wounds, and one day, our paths would cross again. I didn't have a lot to say to justify what I had done, and I thought it was a little selfish to try and force forgiveness on you. But now I see that it would have been more for you than me, and I am truly sorry."

"I know you are, Dad," Juliet said as she squeezed his hand. She could see that his words were true, and she did not feel any of the hate or anger that had once consumed her thoughts of him. Instead, she felt peace. And as he reached out to hug her, she let him. She didn't feel as though she was betraying her mom; she knew that one day soon, they would all be together. And this horrible hurt that had once fractured them would be completely healed.

As she pulled away from her dad, she searched the crowd for Tammy. Suddenly, she just wanted to retreat to a quiet area and regroup.

Right on cue, Tammy appeared and took her hand.

"I'm off to show Juliet the City!" she called with a smile. "You're all invited to my residence for her welcome party tonight. Come when the third rainbow appears."

Juliet was puzzled by her friend's directions but held her hand tight, ready to escape the crowd. She realized she was a bit apprehensive as to what more lay in store for her.

They paused as they approached Avia.

"I will take her on a tour of the City and then we will meet back at her residence?" Tammy proposed to the angelic creature.

"That sounds perfect. Juliet, enjoy the tour!"

As they rounded the corner at the back side of the stadium, Juliet had to stop and take in the sight before her. Just outside of the stadium sat the City. The gates surrounding the City stretched high into the clouds and were comprised completely of an iridescent, pearl-like material. As light reflected on the walls, streams of rainbows flew through the air. In fact, as she looked to the vibrant blue sky, she noticed that there were two massive rainbows making an arch around them. And if she remembered correctly, there were more to come. It was if to signify that here in heaven, God's promises were abundant and never broken.

As they approached the entrance to the City, angels stood guard in front of them. These angels must have been the most fit and trained among their peers; their sinewy, toned physiques were emphasized by their tight grips on the doors to the City. Their wings were the largest Juliet had seen, even making Avia seem tiny in comparison.

"What are they guarding us from?" Juliet asked.

"One day, there will be a last battle. Then, we will all come together to live in the City as one. But you will learn more of that later."

Juliet tensed a bit at the sound of war; she had hoped that once she reached heaven, all the fighting would come to an end.

She didn't have long to dwell on her thoughts; as they were ushered into the gates, she smiled with wonder at all that she saw. In the middle of the city, there were towering skyscrapers that would make earth's largest metropolises seem like small towns. Building after building stretched into the sky; some had the expected rectangular shape, others were oval and even circular in design. The windows on the buildings appeared to all be made of gold and silver, and the city shone like a giant beam of light. It took Juliet's eyes a moment to adjust, but once she did, she noticed stadiums and amphitheaters amongst the hi-rises.

"Are those for sports? Is that a movie theater?"

Somehow, when she'd thought of heaven, she had pictured rows of angelic choirs and a never-ending time of singing and worship to God. She imagined everyone floating on clouds as rotund and cheery angels strummed harps and harmonized.

But here, there was so much that reminded her of earth, only bigger and better. Everything was so clear and refreshing, as though her time on earth had been spent underwater and now she was finally coming up to see things clearly.

"Oh, yes. We have movie theaters, stadiums, coliseums...You won't believe the teams we have here. You used to play basketball right? Wait until you get to fly through the air and slam the ball through the net. It is exhilarating. I'll show you how to join a team in the upcoming opportunities that we have together."

Basketball again? Juliet almost laughed to herself. She hadn't played in ages. But the thought of flying through the air did sound fun. She would have to try.

"And we will have to go to the theater soon. There are so many neat documentaries on earth, with all of the real facts included. Do you want to see how life really began? It's so much more simple than I ever thought!"

Juliet couldn't believe it. Sports and movies in heaven? She noticed a library too. Of course, this library stretched into the clouds and had exterior elevators that you could simply leap aboard to take you to your desired floor. It was truly like nothing she had ever even imagined.

As she looked around the City, Juliet noticed that just outside the center was the most beautiful garden she had ever seen. It was similar to what she thought Hawaii looked like (though she had never been), only more lush and majestic.

There were waterfalls twelve stories high and birds of every different color – even colors she hadn't seen before – soaring through tropical trees that towered above them and disappeared into the clouds above.

Tammy followed her gaze.

"That is Eden. It is such a nice place to go and relax; you can take your journal or your camera and explore. I feel so close to Him there. We will definitely go there as quickly as possible."

Juliet couldn't wait. As she turned her focus back to the City, she noticed a man not too far from her tending a small garden right there in the midst of their urban surroundings. It stood out against the skyscrapers as a mini-retreat in the midst of the busy City.

He felt her smile and looked up to return it.

"Hello and welcome. You must be one of our new members," he said and Juliet nodded.

"How long have you been here?" Juliet asked, trying to make polite conversation.

"That's an excellent question but a hard one to answer. There aren't really days here. I'm sure your friend Tammy will explain how everything works, but each moment seems to run into the next. It is a deeply peaceful thought to know that you don't have to worry about your next breath or feel any urgency to check things off of a to-do list. We will always be here, and no one can separate us from Him or our loved ones."

"You do seem very peaceful," Juliet observed, watching him methodically dig in the dirt to the desired depth and then insert a handful of seeds before massaging the soil back into place.

"Ah, that was not always the case. On earth, my life was the complete opposite. I was a doctor at a large hospital in New York City. Every day, I worried that I would make a mistake and cause someone to die. Everything I did was life or death. It was an extremely hard job, but I was doing what I was supposed to do."

Juliet nodded. She had worked in hospitals and knew the pressures that doctors felt. She felt that same pressure herself, but in the end, the responsibility always came down to the doctor in charge.

He smiled, again radiating that peace that she was beginning to love.

"But here, you see, they don't need doctors. There is no death or pain. My role on earth could not be transferred to heaven. So, I took the skills I had learned in caring for living things and helping them to grow, and then it was clear to me. I should help tend to the gardens. You must go visit Eden; it is a masterpiece."

Juliet promised she would and waved as Tammy led her to the next part of the City.

They rounded a corner, and Juliet noticed a river flowing in the distance, right through the middle of the City.

"What's that?" she asked, and they moved toward it. A moment later, they were standing at its banks.

"This is the River of Life, and it runs through the City and up to His throne room."

Juliet gazed into the swirling depths. It was at once impressive and soothing. In the middle, the water swirled and appeared to go down for quite a ways. A myriad of sea creatures leapt and swam in its fathoms. Dolphins, much larger than she remembered and in all shades of blue, green, and lavender, led the performance. Schools of rainbow-hued fish danced amongst the foaming blue waves. A wall of amber coral poked through on one side, and around the edges of the river, a group of starfish and anemones swayed in the shallows.

As her eyes moved closer to shore, the river seemed to calm a bit, lapping softly at the edge of the green grass that bordered it in on every side.

Near them, a little ways off the bank, a group of angels were in training. Juliet and Tammy approached the crew, and their leader paused as they drew near.

"Welcome, ladies. Everyone, please say hello."

A melodic chorus of greetings welcomed them.

"You must be new," the leader said to Juliet, and she felt her cheeks grow warm. She must have been walking around in a state of awe.

"We are so glad to have you here," he continued. "This new recruit of angels is quite a talented one, and I am enjoying the privilege of training them."

Juliet nodded, but instantly thought it odd that a human would be training a class of angels. She would have thought the angels' knowledge would be much superior to their own.

"It is a wonderful way for us to share knowledge and for me to guide them in their roles. Back on earth, I was able to serve and protect as a police officer. But here, there is no need for that. And so, after I reviewed my skills and goals, this became the obvious choice. And I am loving it."

Juliet smiled. "You seem to be doing a wonderful job," she admired, noting how the angels sat at rapt attention to their instructor.

"Thank you. Please join us again some time."

With promises that she would, Juliet turned to follow Tammy further up the bank.

"There is something I want to show you," she said, taking Juliet's hand. "I remember how much you loved trees, so I thought you would have special appreciation for this."

As they came to the top of a small hill covered in the most amazing red blooms, Juliet saw it.

Towering above them, with branches that reached from one edge of the river to the next, was the Tree of Life. As they stood under it, the light from above was almost completely blocked, and Juliet could admire its extraordinary features. She first noticed a banana-like fruit growing on one edge of the tree, on the other side of the river. Then, right next to that, there was a flowing, grape-type of plant. All in all, she counted at least twelve different types of fruit blossoming from the tree.

"Try one," Tammy said, as she picked an apple-orange amalgamation. With a crispy outer texture and sweet, soft inside that tickled her tongue and enlightened her taste buds, Juliet was enraptured with the new creation.

"It's called apploraniwi, for reasons I am sure you can guess," Tammy said as she grabbed another new fruit from the tree.

They sampled one fruit after another with ever-increasing delight until they reached yet another group of students.

Juliet instantly recognized the face of the man who was teaching them. He had been president of her country for eight years when she was a young girl. He was a revered leader who unified their nation and set the groundwork for countless aid organizations that were still in place when Juliet left earth. He was beloved and almost worshipped around the world as the first and last leader in a long time who seemed to have compassion for everyone.

Juliet was surprised to see him with a handful of young children, reading them a book as the waves of the nearby river lapped softly in the background.

He lifted his head as they approached, and as everyone before him, stopped to welcome them.

"Hello, ladies. Welcome to our class. Today, we are studying the trees and the plants. I thought it was most appropriate to bring them here for our field trip."

His voice was the same as she remembered it, even as a young girl, soft and soothing as it gave authority. The students all happily smiled, and Juliet noticed that they were feasting on the fruit she had sampled earlier.

As the children chatted amongst themselves, Juliet turned to the former president.

"Sir, it is an honor to meet you," she said as she reached out her hand in greeting.

"Ah, the honor is mine," he said and turned to his class. "And here, I have found real honor."

Juliet was puzzled. He had been the most powerful man on earth at one time, and now he was teaching a handful of children.

"I know it does not look like much, but I have the most noble of all jobs. While once I was the leader of nations back on earth, I am now the leader of young minds. What other job could be more important? Here, I am able to instruct and provide knowledge of the greatest truths in the universe. I could not be more blessed."

The soothing, calm voice never wavered, and Juliet trusted him, but still she could not believe that a man with all of his power could be content to teach a simple lesson. She made a mental note to talk with him more as they waved their goodbyes and continued walking.

The surrounding nature was awe-inspiring. Just as she looked from the blossoming trees and flowers by the river, she could turn and view the towering mountains to her right with their snow-capped peaks and promises of fun and adventure. It was as if every season on earth was presented at once, amplified and enhanced to its perfection for their enjoyment.

"Shall we head to your home now?" Tammy asked. Juliet nodded. She knew there was so much more to see, but thankfully, there would be time for that. For now, she looked forward to going home – to seeing what that would be like and to talking more with Avia.

As they walked from the city, a young man with fiery red hair flew past them. Literally, he flew. Juliet watched as he took one step and then bounded into the air at least fifty feet from the ground. He was grinning from ear to ear as he took one giant leap after another.

The women both laughed as they watched him; his smile was contagious and his bright red hair seemed to pop against the blue sky.

"It's as if he's never walked before," Juliet said.

"Yes," Tammy agreed, captivated as well by the young man's jubilant display. "We'll have to learn his story later, but for now, let's get you home. I think there's someone there you'll want to meet."

With the gates of the City behind them, Juliet and Tammy walked through field after field.

As they walked, Juliet noticed a beautiful, dark-skinned woman sitting down in a spot nearby. She was humming the most beautiful melody, and with pure joy on her face, she held a baby in her arms and the hand of a young girl on her right. Juliet noticed that her grip on the baby was tight, as if she had missed the little one for some time and now happily enjoyed their sweet reunion.

As she watched the mother with her children, Juliet again felt her heart tighten. She missed her girls so much that it physically hurt, and she turned to her friend for direction.

"Tammy, how can I ever get over this constant feeling of worry for Ellie and Grace? I miss them more than anyone could ever know," she said and then stopped herself, remembering the plight of her friend. "Do you still miss your children now or does that feeling ever fade away?"

Tammy turned to her and Juliet could see the empathy in her eyes.

"The missing never goes away. Sometimes, it fades; many times, I get wrapped up in everything here. But always, I go back to my family. I check in on them. I pray for them. And I long for that day when we will all be together."

Juliet nodded, hoping that she would soon find some balance in her own emotions as well. Suddenly, another thought hit her.

"One more question, Tammy. Time seems as if it is flying by down on earth, while everything here seems to be going in slow motion. It doesn't add up then; if you only died three earthly years ago, shouldn't you still be going through your own graduation day?"

Tammy nodded, remembering the same confusion she had gone through when she had arrived. There was so much more she had to explain to her friend.

"That's a great question, Juliet. The concept of time here is much different than that on earth. We're not living parallel to them; we're on a completely different plane. It's almost like slow motion and fast forward at the same time. What feels like one minute in heaven and five years on earth is actually just a millisecond in heaven. Things happen here at warp speed; since the moment you arrived, it's only been like the blink of an eye. You are experiencing everything at an earth-like pace, but it's actually happening much, much quicker. How else could we welcome more than a hundred thousand new graduates each earthly day?"

As they rounded a corner, Juliet wanted to continue talking about the subject, to understand more fully, but Tammy stopped and touched her hand.

"Here it is," she said, and paused with excitement. "Here is your residence."

Juliet turned her attention to the house in front of her. The first thing she noticed was the massive tree that was featured in the front yard. Part oak, part maple, and part peach tree, this large creation was beyond her dreams. She loved the way its branches stretched like arms waiting to welcome her and anyone that might visit. She loved the cool cover provided by the dense leaves. And, as she picked a peach and sampled it, she loved the refreshing fruit.

Her eyes were then drawn to the home itself. Set back from the tree but still under its shade, a huge wraparound porch presented the perfect place for a relaxing late afternoon tea or morning coffee. Was there coffee here? Juliet couldn't wait to find out.

The pale green exterior was soothing and Juliet soon found herself at the front door, eager to enter.

"Go ahead, go inside," Tammy said and they both walked in.

The main living area was large and comfortable with neutral furnishings. There were no decorations on the floor or coverings on the windows. Basically, it was a blank canvas.

"You'll be able to decorate it as you wish later," Tammy said and Juliet felt excited with the possibilities. But even as she considered what she might do, a sadness overwhelmed her. She would be living in this house all alone; there was no family to share this amazing abode with. She knew that she had plenty of extended family and friends here, but it still wasn't the same. She needed her family with her.

They walked slowly down the hallway and made their way to the kitchen.

There, sitting at the large wooden table that anchored the room was Avia, and in her arms lay a tiny, sleeping baby.

When Juliet saw the child, her breath left her. The dark hair, the soft features, the green and gold eyes. She looked so much like Ellie. She couldn't help herself as she reached out to touch her delicate cheek.

The baby breathed deeply and did not stir. Without hesitation, Avia handed the infant to Juliet. The baby fit snuggly in her arms.

"Can you hold this little one for me? We have much to discuss."

"Of course," Juliet said, already intoxicated by that innocent and clean baby smell. She nuzzled her cheek. She was so captivated she could only smile as Tammy headed out the back door.

"See you at the third rainbow. Avia will show you the way," Tammy said as she left.

Juliet turned back to Avia, ready to hear more.

"Let's get comfortable," she said, and they both headed to the den area. Juliet eased into a soft couch, cuddling the baby in her arms. Avia sat across from her and began to talk; Juliet tried to listen.

"I am only going to share with you the information you need to make it through your beginning time here. There will be so much to learn, and the rest will come in its own time.

First, you will begin your time in heaven reviewing and learning. You will consider all that you did on earth, focusing on those things that you loved and that properly displayed your gifts. At the same time, you are welcome to visit the libraries and movie theaters to learn more about our expansive universe: the past, the present and the future. You can take classes and sit in on lectures. Your options are endless."

Juliet focused on the melodic words. She knew she would need to find a new career; nursing was obviously a job that had no use here in heaven. But, nurturing and servitude had their place anywhere, and she looked forward to finding a new role that made good use of those skills.

"As you continue to learn and choose your roles here in heaven, you will have much direction. You always have access to Him, and I can provide answers to any questions you may have. Also, just talking to anyone that you meet provides a great learning opportunity."

Juliet nodded in agreement, thinking of the people that she had met today and how much they had taught her.

"Of course, your most important role will have to do with this little one," Avia said, nodding towards the baby.

Juliet held her close and held her breath even tighter.

"You mean, I will get to care for this baby?" she asked, instantly excited by the possibility. A little life to nurture; a new part of her family. Inexplicably, she felt connected to this beautiful little girl.

"She is your main responsibility, Juliet. I am pleased to introduce you to your granddaughter, Julianne."

13 / ELLIE AT THIRTY

Ellie set the test on the back of the toilet and walked into the bedroom to check the clock. She'd give it three minutes, one extra just to be sure.

Please, please, let it be positive, she pleaded heavenward. But she doubted there was anyone listening. Ellie didn't know if she could handle another negative result. Ever since they had lost Julianne, she had been rigorous and methodic about trying to get pregnant again, reducing the getting-pregnant-process to almost a science—which in fact it was. The more she read about pregnancy, the more she realized that every baby that was born was truly a miracle. And that's what she needed right now.

Ben had been so supportive throughout everything. He had mourned with her when Julianne was lost; he had been sure not to rush her to try again, but now as the time passed, she could tell even he was getting frustrated. It seemed like couples all around them were having babies. Grace was about to have her third child, Laynie had two, but Ellie still couldn't produce one.

As she waited for the results to appear, Ellie headed back to the only room where she strangely found peace. Julianne's nursery was saturated in the most soft and feminine pink. Though she had never been a girly girl, the moment that Ellie discovered she was expecting a little girl, she became obsessed with the color. The frilly pink dresses that had seemed so silly only months before were instantly purchased and hung in the closet, awaiting a little princess to try on each one.

And just as Julianne's impending presence had inspired a change in her taste of fashion, it also completely revolutionized Ellie's views on motherhood.

For the longest time, she hadn't even wanted to be a mom. The thought of having another little life to care for, to worry about, to stress over, just wasn't something she wanted to take on. In fact, it caused her palms to sweat and her stomach to turn in knots whenever they talked about it.

And Ben talked about it a lot. Almost right after they got married, he got a sly gleam in his eye and started calling her little mama. It took three years for him to convince her she could handle that title.

Even then, they hadn't really been trying as much as not preventing it. Ellie still wasn't one hundred percent sure this was what she wanted, though Ben was convinced that she would fall in love with the idea once it happened. And he had been so right.

That made the day of Julianne's birth that much more excruciating. Ellie was eight months along, essentially full term, when something hadn't felt right. She and Julianne had a morning ritual established. Once Ellie woke up and sat down for breakfast, Julianne would kick a little hello as soon as the food hit Ellie's system. That morning, however, Ellie's womb was strangely still. After eating, she found some orange juice and drank a full glass. She'd read once that the sugary sweet jolt could help a quiet fetus spring back into action.

After a few minutes, there was still no movement. Ellie was trying to remain calm; she didn't want to overreact or even consider that her worst nightmare might be coming true. But somehow in her heart, she knew even then that it was.

***

The girl was fourteen, almost fifteen, and she could no longer hide the pregnancy. She'd been wearing overly baggy clothes for three months now, when her normally thin figure had ballooned past the point of a little weight gain. She was terrified of the upcoming confrontation with her parents. How could she explain it to them? She didn't have any answers. Just a simple mistake made when no one was around to tell her no. And she never thought it could happen after just one time.

But her changing body and the pregnancy test she bought at a drugstore while supposedly purchasing bread and milk for her mom confirmed it all.

At school, she was the perfect student. She aced all of the tests; all of the teachers selected her for special errands. Most of the kids wanted to be her friend. But at home, she was nobody. Long ago, she had realized that bringing home an A on a test would garner little to no reaction from her mom. She was too consumed with her own friends and her own projects.

She rarely saw her dad. He worked all of the time, and when he was home, the last thing he wanted to do was sit and talk to her about her life. He wanted to fall into his recliner and get lost in some ball game and the drink in his right hand.

But she still continued to try and excel in every way that she could. She hadn't lost hope that one day her parents would take the time to notice, and when they did, she wanted them to be proud.

Though her family was oblivious, she had been attracting attention of a different sort lately. Last summer, she had officially become a woman, as the school nurse had said. The changes had provided her with much notice from her classmates, specifically the boys.

A major sleepover party at a friend's house had been the scene of the irreversible error. The most popular girls had all been there, and once the lights went out, a handful of boys quietly crashed the party. One of the boys that every girl giggled over picked her and kissed her roughly. Before she had time to protest, he moved along. Not wanting to stand out from the friends that accepted her and made her feel welcome, she had said nothing. She hadn't really known what was going on, and before she knew it had begun, it was over.

The party had been the talk of the school for weeks. At first, it seemed like everyone had made the same mistake she had, but the more she listened, the more she realized it was all talk. In fact, it appeared she was the only one who had actually let her aggressor go all the way.

When she starting feeling sick every morning a couple of months later and her body ached in ways that it never had, she thought she had the flu. But after a few days home from school without a lessening of her symptoms, she started to get worried.

That's when she'd headed out to the drug store a few blocks away to run errands for her mom…and to purchase the most important test of her life. Unfortunately, she hadn't passed this one.

The double pink lines brought a terror to her heart that she had never felt before. She had worked so hard to make her parents proud, and now, before they even had a chance to, she would be a disappointment to them.

This crushed her spirit, and so she had hid it from them. There was no friend at school that she trusted with the secret; it was hers alone to bear.

She started eating a lot more, or at least creating an impression that provided a reason for her puffy face and swelling ankles. She wore baggy clothes and ran the shower when she had to throw up. She never went to the doctor but started taking some multi-vitamins she found in the cabinet. Surely those would provide some nourishment for the baby.

All alone with her decisions, she still hadn't decided what she should do with the baby. She knew she couldn't keep it; she knew she didn't want it. She most certainly knew that her family would have nothing to do with it. It would be an embarrassment to them, and that was something that she wanted less than anything.

And so, still without a plan, she was standing at her locker one morning when a gush of liquid soaked her shoes and socks.

***

On the day that Julianne would come, Ellie had tried to call Ben on his cell phone, but there was no answer. He had mentioned meetings that morning at the fire hall, but now Ellie couldn't recall the details.

She debated calling her sister for advice but knew she would probably just laugh her off. Grace would dismiss her fears just as she had many times before during this pregnancy when Ellie had worried about a cramp or a bump.

"Ellie, pregnancy is a natural thing. There is a ninety-nine percent chance that everything will be just fine. Just let it happen, and stop worrying."

Somehow, Ellie had defied the odds her whole life, and she was beginning to realize it was happening again.

Without care for how silly she might look, Ellie hopped in her car and sped to her OB/GYN's office.

Forty-five minutes later, she was hooked up to every machine possible and being wheeled in for an emergency C-section. Ben was on the way but he wouldn't arrive until later, when Ellie was still cradling the lifeless body of their stillborn daughter.

Ellie felt those same hot tears streaming down her cheeks now, as she held the extra soft pink lamb she had bought for Julianne and stared around the beautiful room that was only missing one thing. She knew the pregnancy test would be negative. She knew that for some reason, this happiness was never meant to be hers.

As she walked back into the bathroom, the glaringly empty second box on the test was waiting to meet her. She picked up the test and shook it, hoping desperately that somehow, the little pink line would appear. But it never did. And Ellie knew it never would.

***

The girl dashed to the closest bathroom, desperately hoping that no one in the hallway had noticed her sloshing footprints. Luckily, most of her classmates were heading to their next class, and the bathroom was empty. She quickly ran to the last stall.

She closed the lid and sat on one of the toilets, beginning to breathe quickly and gripping her stomach. Was this happening? She wasn't even sure how far along she was. Maybe 37 or 38 weeks? She had meant to try and count that morning, but she avoided doing that whenever possible. It just reminded her of the fact that she was going to have to face this secret sooner rather than later. And she just didn't know what to do.

Her intense breathing continued, and she wondered if she should go to the nurse for help. But no, she couldn't do that. The nurse would call her parents, and she was going to do everything possible to avoid that. Even if it meant she died. At least then she wouldn't have to face them.

She stayed in the bathroom all morning until the regular cramps began. They started softly, just a tightening in her lower abdomen that made it hard to breathe for a moment and brought a flush to her cheeks. Then, they started coming more regularly. Soon, it seemed like she was tightening like that every couple of minutes.

Then, the pressure began. It was an intense desire to push that she could not ignore. She stood up off the toilet and squatted down. She prayed that no one would come into the bathroom. She prayed that she would not die. She prayed that somehow, this baby would not be born.

And then, as the shrill bell rang to signify the beginning of fifth period, another shrill sound could be heard echoing through the hallways. A moment later, the soft muted cries of a baby joined them.

***

Ben found Ellie in Julianne's room when he got home from work. He knew she would be in there. He'd taken off early because she hadn't returned his calls or emails all afternoon. He worried sometimes that she would take this desire to be a mother too far and let the depression and guilt she felt for not being successful overwhelm her. He prayed every day for their miracle and had to admit his discouragement when it did not come. Somehow, he knew there was something in store for them, something great, but it had yet to appear. And if Ellie was teetering on the edge of despair, he was doing his best not to join her. One of them had to stay strong, and he knew his wife had been through so much already. He owed it to her to stand by her through this.

As he walked in and found Ellie in the rocking chair, singing softly to a stuffed bear that had been a gift from his parents, he knew that his fears were not far off. He touched her back softly, trying not to startle her. But she didn't react to his presence. She just continued to rock and sing a lullaby he recognized from his childhood.

"Did you take another test, Ellie? It's okay, honey. It's going to take some time. The doctor says it could take another year to get pregnant, and that would be completely normal. Please, don't worry. It will happen. We will find a way."

Still no reaction from Ellie. His beautiful wife that had fought so many battles and overcome so many demons in her path was finally giving in. He wasn't going to let it happen without a fight of his own. Ellie rocked and rocked, minutes passing by as he stood by patiently, waiting for the daydream to end. Finally, he couldn't take it anymore; he couldn't let her slip any further from reality. He pulled the bear from her hands and stood in front of her.

"Ellie, please look at me," he said with a quiet desperation.

She did look at him then, but it was with a look of horror and anger, as though he had ripped a living child from her hands.

"What are you doing, Ben?" she asked. And then he realized she was still in the middle of her fantasy. Slowly, he could see the stuffed animal fade from their beautiful Julianne back into an inanimate object. And then the defeat returned to Ellie's eyes.

She turned away from him and he could see her shoulders droop and her breathing slow as she came back to reality. What was happening to her? Was she losing her mind?

He touched her arm again gently, and she let him take her into an embrace. He held her for minutes without saying a word. He let her cry and cried himself. This frustration, this loss…he did not want her to suffer any more. He wanted to protect her and keep the pain away. He would do whatever it took.

"I knew this would happen," Ellie whispered. "I was so happy; I allowed myself to believe it was okay, and I finally relaxed. I am so sorry that I did this to us," she said through clenched teeth and broken sobs.

"This is not your fault," Ben whispered back as he held her, but he knew she would not listen to him. He knew she did not believe it.

He closed his eyes and cried out to God in his heart…the God who had always heard him before but seemed to be strangely silent on this issue that was ripping them apart. He pleaded for their miracle; he begged for mercy. And he had faith that somehow, He would provide a solution. He just wished his wife shared his confidence.

"We will figure this out, Ellie," he said as he rubbed her dark hair and continued to hold her tight. "We can do this together. We will have our child somehow. I promise you, you will be rocking a baby in this chair very soon."

***

The girl took off her jacket and cradled it around the squirming, oozing mess in her arms. How could people say that babies were so cute? This was honestly the most disgusting thing she had ever seen.

Still unsure of what to do, and feeling incredibly weak and beyond tired, she held the baby for a couple of hours until she felt she could move.

All afternoon, people had come in and out of the bathroom, and she had just prayed that the baby would be quiet. Luckily, the baby had been silent.

Still unsure of what to do, she heard the loud wail of a fire truck about midway through seventh period. The sound startled her into reality, and that's when her plan finally began to take shape. She just had to wait until the school closed down for the night to make her move.

14 / THE WAVES

Avia watched Juliet as she gently rocked the infant in her arms. She hadn't seen Juliet look this peaceful and happy since her arrival. Avia was hesitant to interrupt this quiet moment, but she knew Juliet had many questions that needed to be answered.

"I wanted to share with you more of your story. Each action on earth is like a pebble tossed into a body of water. The ripples that occur because of it are almost beyond measure. Sometimes, those ripples are so massive, they become waves. Do you want to see the blessings that occurred because of your death?"

Juliet nodded. Though she was still captivated with the sleeping bundle in her arms, she was very interested in hearing how that one act of carelessness and tragedy could be shown in a positive light.

Avia smiled. "These are just a few of the lives that were changed because of your accident and death. And as you will see, most of them grew into powerful waves of reaction that blessed countless others in their wake."

Avia nodded to a large TV screen in the middle of the living room.

"Sit back, relax, and enjoy the show!" she said, and Juliet turned her attention to the monitor that was beginning to display the day of her death.

She recognized the crash site, and the image quickly zoomed in to the handful of vehicles that had been involved in the pileup. She saw her car, mangled and smoking. She tried to see herself inside of the mess, but the screen focused instead on one of the EMT vehicles already parked on the outskirts of the accident.

A little boy and his mom were sitting in the rear of the truck, receiving treatment from a technician. Juliet suddenly caught her breath. Did someone die because of her wreck? She had never even considered the possibility of injuring someone else, or even killing someone, because of her momentary negligence.

But everyone in the vehicle seemed to be very much alive. The mother was hugging tightly onto her son as the paramedic examined him. There was a small cut on the boy's forehead, and as that was being attended to, he answered a few questions.

"How many fingers am I holding up?" the paramedic asked, and when he quickly switched from one to two to four fingers, the boy slowly grinned.

The paramedic could tell that the boy was frightened and wanted to try and make him relax. At first glance, nothing appeared to be wrong, but he was thorough at his job and wanted to ensure nothing got past him. That was his worst fear.

As he did a quick examination of the boy's extremities, he noticed that he flinched with light pressure to his abdomen.

"Do you remember where you got this bruise?" the paramedic asked, pointing to a large whelp on the inside of the boy's arm.

The boy shrugged his shoulders.

"Did you get that from a baseball, Joey? I think that's what you told me," the mom said, and the boy shrugged his shoulders again.

"And this bruise?" the paramedic pointed to another black and blue area on the boy's left knee.

"I don't know," Joey said. "Maybe from another baseball?"

"My son is very active, sir. Lately, he seems to be bruising all over. But that's just normal for a boy. He runs and jumps and tumbles all over the place. Just like any other six year old."

The mother visibly stiffened with the continued questions, and as the paramedic continued to identify bruises on the boy's body, it became clear that he felt something was wrong. The mother tensed again and held her boy tighter.

"Ma'am, have you noticed any changes in Joey lately? Has he been eating normally and playing outside as much as he normally does?"

"Of course," she snapped. And then, he could see her stop to think. "Well, actually, for the past couple of weeks, he just hasn't been finishing his dinner. And we missed a couple of soccer games because he was too tired to play."

"Uh huh…" the paramedic said as he made notes on his clipboard.

The mother's eyes grew large.

"But it's not like he's depressed or anything. Joey is a very happy boy!"

The paramedic was still nodding and continued to write without meeting the mother's eyes.

She sat up straighter and her voice grew louder.

"Do you hear me? Joey is happy! We are not abusing our son!"

The paramedic looked up at her quickly.

"Oh no, ma'am. I didn't think that. I can tell you love your son. But I think we need to do a few more tests. Would it be okay if we take him on to the hospital? I just want to rule out a few things before I release you."

Instantly, the defensiveness and anger from Joey's mom were replaced with fear and uncertainty.

"Of course," she said. "Let's go right away."

Moments later, the EMT vehicle left the scene of the accident and drove to the nearby children's hospital.

Joey was admitted and blood tests were administered. Joey's father met them at the hospital during the process, and for

Graduation Day

hours, the three of them sat in a hospital room. Joey sat and played with the toy cars his dad brought with him and tried not to look at his parents. His mom had tears in her eyes that wouldn't go away, and the wrinkle in the middle of his dad's forehead that appeared when he was really upset seemed etched in his face.

Finally, after darkness had settled at the hospital, a doctor entered the room. He shook hands with Joey's parents and had them sit down in the small and uncomfortable chairs across the room from Joey's bed.

He talked for a few minutes and then Joey's mom hung her head. The tears that had been threatening all day long began to fall and she buried her face in her husband's shoulder. Joey's dad took a deep breath and began to ask questions.

Later, when the doctor had left and Joey's dad had gone to get some dinner for everyone from the hospital cafeteria, Joey looked at his mom.

"Mom, did I hear it right?" he asked.

"What, honey? What did you hear?" she stalled, searching her mind for the right words to say. The doctor had just dropped this bomb on them and they hadn't had time to process it, let alone discuss how to explain it to Joey. She wished her husband would hurry up and get back. He always knew the right thing to say.

"Did the doctor say I might have cancer? Does that mean I am going to die?"

Joey's mom closed her eyes. She wanted to scream "No! You are not going to die! We are going to fight this! We are not going to lose you!" But she didn't know if any of that was true. In fact, she felt like she didn't know anything at all. How could she have missed the signs? How could she not have known that her son had a horrible disease? If they hadn't had the accident, she most likely wouldn't have taken him to the doctor until his next scheduled checkup six months away. It was a miracle they were even in the hospital. The doctor had mentioned that early detection is one of the keys to a successful treatment, and so she was so thankful for the pile up this morning. She would gladly have someone crash into her car any time if it meant she had a greater chance of saving her son.

Joey was still looking at her, waiting for an answer.

"Joey, your dad and I love you, and we are going to be right here with you as we figure this all out. No matter what happens, we are going to take care of you. Everything is going to be okay."

She had to add that last part in there, because even if she didn't know for sure that everything was going to turn out alright, she wanted him to believe that it would. The answer seemed to pacify him, and he turned back to his toy cars as his dad entered the room with a tray filled with food. They were all happy for the distraction.

Juliet watched the scene with tears in her eyes. One of her greatest nightmares had always been that one of her daughters would get sick. Or that Mark would get sick. Cancer was a true monster that ravaged everything in its path. Her heart ached for that poor family and the nightmare that was beginning for them.

The screen showed images of Joey's treatment. Juliet noticed his hair quickly fell out; his skin color faded to a dingy pallor; and he spent more and more days at the hospital. Poor Joey seemed to get much, much worse before he began to get better. But, somewhere in the midst of all that nausea and pain of his treatments, Joey did begin to get better.

Soon, they were celebrating Joey's seventh birthday. A large group of people surrounded the little guy who was proudly sporting a buzz cut. He kept running his fingers over it, still surprised that he could feel his own hair again. He blew out the candles and everyone cheered.

As his mom began cutting the cake and passing it around to the guests, his dad leaned over to him.

"Did you remember to make a wish, Joey?" he asked, still so thankful to see his son happy and well.

"Of course, Dad! I know I'm not supposed to tell you, but I want you to know. I wished that one day I would be able to help people the same way the doctors helped me. I want to save lives."

His dad pulled him close for a hug and they both laughed, giddy to be together. Each moment was a precious one.

Joey would never forget that feeling or that wish. He worked hard all throughout school, always so grateful for his life. He lived as though he had been given bonus time on this earth, and he wanted to make the most of it. Graduating with honors from his high school, he attended a well-respected college for his undergraduate studies and then moved on to receive his PhD. Though at first he wanted to be a doctor so that he could help patients directly, he soon learned that he had a passion for the science behind the diseases. And the cures.

Juliet saw Joey in research labs, hovering over a microscope, scrawling on a white board, administering trials. She saw him making presentations to colleagues, visiting hospitals, and scribbling note after note late into the night.

She also saw him talking with a young woman who looked at him with affection in her eyes. Though his free time was limited, he soon began spending it almost exclusively with her. A wedding appeared; love and joy radiated from the ceremony and there was not a dry eye in the house as Joey's parents toasted the happy couple during the reception. Soon, a young baby joined their family and then another. Two more lives with endless opportunities stretching before them.

In the final scene, Joey was attending an awards banquet. His wife and boys sat around him at the head table. Speeches were made; applause could be heard. Joey accepted a plaque for his achievements in the fight against cancer. One of his clinical trials had proven successful. Lives had been saved; diseases had been erased. A large screen at the banquet displayed the faces of the children who had been the recipients of his research and dedication. As the crowd cheered, Juliet's screen faded to black.

She turned to Avia and smiled.

"Amazing," she breathed.

"It is so incredible how one thing leads to another and then another. Little actions bring great consequences. Some good, some bad. But it is truly a gift to see how the bad can become good."

"It is such a relief and a blessing to see that there is a bright side to all of the sadness," Juliet agreed.

"And there is more...let's watch," Avia said, and they both turned back to the screen.

Again, they were at the scene of the accident. Paramedics were scrambling everywhere. They first focused their attention on the city bus that Juliet had hit; it was filled with the most people and the most screaming.

As the paramedics began their job, the screen zoomed in on two teenagers who had been riding their bikes home from the convenience store and witnessed the accident. Amber, who would be entering her senior year of high school in the fall, stood in awe. The straw to her extra large diet soda was still halfway to her lips, frozen as the scene unfolded before her.

The first set of emergency responders slowly started removing people from the city bus. A commotion of bleeding and yelling created a sense of chaos, but Amber noticed that the paramedics moved about their jobs very methodically. It was as though the swirl of activity and pain around them could not break through their focus.

First, a little girl whose arm was hanging at an awkward angle received treatment. A gentle assessment was made and a sling was placed before the little girl boarded the ambulance to be transported to the hospital for further x-rays.

Countless others were bandaged, sutured, and re-assured that everything was okay. Amber couldn't stop watching one of the paramedics, a woman in her late thirties whose short brown pony tail swung back and forth as she ran from one injury to the next. She comforted crying children and tended to the elderly. She bandaged grown men who were trying not to look afraid.

"She's awesome," Amber whispered to her friend who had been ready to head home for the past ten minutes.

"Who?" her friend asked, more focused on eating her sticky bun than on anything at the accident scene.

"That lady paramedic. She has been working non-stop since she got here. Since we've been watching, she's already helped like ten people. How awesome is that?"

Amber's friend didn't look too impressed.

"Haven't you ever seen St. Elsewhere?"

Amber shot her a look.

"Of course. But this is different. This is real. I've never seen anything like this."

"Yeah, it's awesome. Ready to go?"

Amber sighed and looked at her friend. She was about to concede and turn her bike back towards home when another ambulance arrived. These emergency workers jumped out and, after quickly determining that the city bus and additional cars had been taken care of, they approached Juliet's car.

Juliet held her breath as she watched the screen. Somewhere inside, she hoped that they would save her. But as they attempted to revive her, it was soon obvious that their efforts were in vain. One of the paramedics noted her time of death and placed a sheet over her.

Juliet felt her heart fall, though she'd already known the outcome. The screen again zoomed in on Amber. Her eyes were wide and she was fidgeting nervously on her bicycle seat.

"Oh my goodness, did you see that?" she hissed to her friend.

"What? Another bloody nose?"

"No! That lady died!" She tried to remain calm, but something inside her was catching fire. This amazing display of life and death and courage among chaos stayed with her for the rest of the day. Long after her friend had gone home and they had retold the story countless times to their family and friends, Amber kept thinking about what she saw. She had never been so captivated by something. Even ballet.

Amber had been training to be a ballerina since she was three years old. When her mom had first slipped that pink tutu over her head and laced up her pointy shoes, they had both giggled with excitement.

For years, it was something they had cherished together. Hour after hour of practice, recital after recital, outfit after outfit. The amount of effort and time ballet had consumed was amazing. But Amber had loved every step of the way.

Mostly, she had loved the time it allowed her to spend with her mom. As the youngest of four children, time with her mom was scarce. There was always someone who needed help with homework or someone who had a soccer game to attend. Their house was non-stop with activity. Often, Amber would go days without stopping to talk with her mom, to have a real conversation and not just a quick peck on the cheek and a cursory "how was your day?"

Amber knew her parents loved her, but she was still thankful that her mom took her to practice every Thursday night at the studio. Though she had long ago gotten her license and now went to practice multiple nights a week, the Thursday night habit that had started when she was a little girl had never been abandoned. And Amber was thankful for that. It was on those car rides that she confessed her first kiss, her most secret worries, and her deepest fears.

Now, as Amber lay in bed after her very exciting day, she thought about the drive with her mother for the next ballet practice. She had much to talk about: shared dreams that may get put on hold and new dreams that may change her focus and plans for the future. She had already received a full scholarship proposal to Juilliard, and she was simply filling out the necessary forms for acceptance. There had never been a question if she would go.

Until now. Until she had seen a glimpse of something so powerful, so inspiring, so important that she couldn't get it out of her mind. Maybe there was more to life than just dance. As much as she loved it, she was suddenly gripped with the conviction that something else was expected from her.

She slipped out of bed and knelt beside the white ruffly sheets that had snuggled her to sleep since she was a young girl. She bowed her head and closed her eyes. She didn't know exactly what to say. God had answered her prayers with the miraculous scholarship opportunity. That had been beyond her wildest dreams. Her whole family was so proud of her. But now, all she could think about was becoming something she had never before been interested in. She wasn't even that strong in math or science.

Amber was still kneeling by her bed when her mom came in to check in on her an hour later, though she had long since fallen asleep. Her eyes had gotten heavy as she had tried to voice her confusion and tried to make sense of her conflicting desires. Her mom helped her into bed and kissed her cheek.

Time at school went by quickly and soon, Amber was packing her tights and ballet shoes and grabbing her bag as her mom waited in the car. As they drove, they talked and talked and talked. At first, her mom was quiet when she revealed her thoughts.

"This is a very important decision, Amber. A scholarship to Juilliard is not something to be taken lightly. You've worked so hard for so long. And you were obviously born for ballet. You are such a natural. You always have been."

Amber nodded. She had expected a bit of resistance. And now she hoped for understanding as she tried to explain exactly how moved she had been by the wreck and all that she had seen, how desperately she wanted to be the one running to those in need and have the knowledge to help them.

But her mom never quite expressed the understanding she had expected.

"We'll talk more after you practice," she said, cutting Amber off during her explanation. The rest of the ride was in silence, and Amber worried that her mother was angry.

After practice was over, she slid into the car and waited for her mom to bring up the discussion, but she never did. The whole way home she talked about everything but what Amber wanted to discuss. And Amber let it go. As they got out of the car and headed into their home, her mother touched her shoulder.

"Have you reconsidered what you were talking about?" she asked softly, and Amber could hear the almost desperate ache in her voice. She knew that her mother had once wanted to be a dancer and that part of what they shared was a culmination of both of their dreams. As the only daughter, the weight was on her shoulders to make it happen. For so long, there had been no question, and this life had been anything but a burden.

But as she nodded to her mom and watched her smile, deeply relieved, she now felt a stifling dread and knew that a tough decision would have to be made.

Flashes of images appeared on the screen in front of Juliet. Amber at school, laughing with her friends. Amber at ballet recitals, with her mom cheering her on. Amber walking across the stage and accepting her diploma. Amber packing her bag and riding in the car with her mom once more, this time as she moved across the country to begin her time at Juilliard.

Then, the images were much the same: ballet practice, ballet recital; Amber was living and breathing her dream, but it all felt so empty. Knowing she should be so happy, Amber felt incredible guilt as she slowly began to dread waking up every day. Suddenly, everything she had ever wanted seemed pointless.

When she headed home for Christmas break, Amber tried to seem happy for her family. She knew they were so proud of her. Day after day, she worked to put a smile on her face, and each night she would curl up in her old bed and wish she could stay there forever.

One night, when she thought everyone was asleep, she knelt again by her bed and the tears began to flow. She tried to keep her cries quiet, but when she heard her door open, she knew she had not been successful. Her mom entered slowly and put her arms around Amber's shoulders.

"Please, honey, tell me what's wrong. Has it been hard being so far away? We've missed you so much too. But it will get easier. Have you been making any friends?"

Amber found it difficult to speak. Her lips just quivered when she tried to get the words out.

"I promise, Amber. It will all get easier. You have worked too hard to give up now," her mom said, and hugged her tightly.

Amber closed her eyes and let her mom hold her close. They stayed that way for minutes that turned into an hour, until finally Amber's eyes began to close. And just as she had done countless times as a child, she fell asleep in her mother's arms.

She left home a few days later and headed back to school with promises to call more often and to try and make more friends.

The next semester was much the same, and when Spring Break finally came, Amber had made her decision. Her mother met her at the door, and once again, Amber could see the desperate need in her eyes to know that everything was okay.

They sat right there on the porch and Amber poured her heart out. This time, her mom listened. Soon, the screen was filled with different images. Amber at a night school, beginning to take paramedic classes. Hours of CPR training, anatomy lessons, and physiology classes.

There were many days when she studied and studied and wondered if she had made the biggest mistake of her life. But when she passed the state exam and became an official paramedic, Amber knew the joy she felt inside proved it was all worth it.

The screen then showed the differences that Amber would make with her life: the patients that she would encourage; the injuries that she would help heal; the lives that she would save.

Juliet saw each face and breathed deeply. Because of that one day, the incident that she had caused, all the pain that she had brought, a girl had decided to change her life to help take all that away from others.

"That was a beautiful story, Avia. What a tough road that young girl had to take to finally do what she was meant to do. And to think that my accident was the spark that set it all in motion."

"Absolutely. A very timely occurrence that she was put in place to see. Ready for one more?"

Juliet nodded and settled back with little Julianne to watch.

The next scene before them was quite different than the other two. They were led into a kitchen, where a woman with graying hair was fixing breakfast. One pan sizzled with bacon and another was prepared for French toast. Juliet could almost smell the delicious aromas she knew filled that home. The woman wore an apron around her loose dress, one that was slightly faded and had most likely been around for many years. As she turned and headed to the counter to begin plating her dishes, Juliet could see that the woman had kind eyes. She wondered what effect her death could possibly have had on this stranger.

A moment later, a man entered the room. He was heavy set, and his hair was much grayer than his wife's, receding quite a bit at the hairline. He walked into the kitchen and sat at his seat.

"Breakfast is almost ready, dear," came his wife's cheerful voice. "How did you sleep last night?"

"Fine," he mumbled, not looking up. He sat for a moment and then became agitated. He looked around the table.

"Where is the paper?" he demanded.

"Oh! Right here!" the wife said, jumping at his request and quickly retrieving the newspaper from the living room. "I wanted to show you something."

She pulled out the Metro section and opened the paper to an article on the second page.

"Take a look at this," she said and handed him his prized paper.

Juliet strained to see the article and thought she could see images of a traffic incident.

The man read for a moment and then looked at her. It was amazing that he could be such a grouch and his wife so kind.

"What? I don't see anything. Just some wreck down south."

"Isn't that the area of town your brother lives in?" she asked quietly and turned back to her preparations.

He was still for a minute and then looked at her closely.

"Why did you have to bring that up? You know I don't want to talk about it."

"It's been fifteen years, Sam. Don't you think it's time you returned his phone calls? He's all you've got, besides me. And I'm getting old. Why don't you give him a call?"

Her pleas were soft and quiet; it was obviously a subject that she hated to broach, but one that she felt she had to.

She offered him a plate full of mouthwatering breakfast as a peace offering. He pushed it away without looking and rose from the table.

"Not hungry," he said and walked from the room.

His wife sighed and picked up the plate. She put plastic wrap around it and placed it in the refrigerator. He would be hungry soon; she knew her Sam could never resist a good meal.

Unfortunately, that was the only thing about her Sam that was remotely like the man she had married. Ever since the falling out with his brother almost two decades ago, Sam had become a grouchy, inconsiderate man who seemed to have little regard for her feelings or anyone else's. They rarely did anything as a couple, and now that he was retired, he simply moped around the house all day, picking fights whenever he could and making her life miserable.

She was tired of it. She had put up with it long enough, and this was the last straw. If he wanted to live the rest of his life angry and mean and hateful, that was fine. But she wanted no part of it.

Suddenly, with a determination she hadn't felt in years, she left the kitchen and headed straight into her bedroom. She had her own room and her own closet; they hadn't shared those things for as long as she could remember.

She began to fill her suitcase with her favorite clothes; there were a handful of outfits that she really wanted to keep. Then, she added in all of the necessities. She was putting together her toiletry bag when Sam walked in the door.

"What's all this commotion about?" he asked and then noticed what she was doing. "Are we going somewhere? Did you forget to tell me?"

Calmly and with resolve, she looked up at him. "*We* aren't going anywhere. I am leaving you. I have had enough of your horrible attitude. I've called my sister and she is setting up a room for me there. I can stay as long as I need to. And I don't plan to return."

Sam stood there, and for the first time she could remember, he didn't have anything to say. His eyes just kept getting bigger and bigger, but before long, anger began to take over the surprise.

"You're going where? To your sister's? Are you crazy? Your home is with me. We are married, and we have been for the past thirty-three years."

"And I have been unhappy for the past fifteen. I've tried to talk to you about this, but it's not worth it any more. Why do you even want me here? You just grumble at me and slam doors and stomp off to the garage. You can do that just fine all by yourself."

"Mary, let's talk about this later, honey," he said, his tone softening. She looked up at his term of endearment. He hadn't used any words like that in a long time. But fifteen years of misery could not be overcome by one kind remark.

She picked up her bags and walked towards the bedroom door.

"I'll be at my sister's. When you call your brother and make up with him, you can call me. Until then, I don't want to hear that mean old voice of yours."

And with that, she left the house and a very shocked Sam in her wake.

It took him two weeks to finally call his brother. By then, there was no clean laundry in the house and he was tired of TV dinners and fast food. And he missed his wife. He missed her sweet voice and her laugh. How could he have been so stupid?

The call with his brother was a short one. He demanded an apology and when he didn't get one, he slammed down the phone. Didn't his brother realize he was doing him a favor? The little punk had cheated him out of a once-in-a-lifetime deal when their parents passed away about fifteen years before.

When they were dividing up the estate, his little brother had begged him for the house. He had gone on and on about how much it meant to him and how many wonderful memories he had from when they were growing up. It was a house he wanted to share with his children and pass on through the generations. Sam and Mary didn't have any children, and it was an emotional time. Sam felt compelled to do the right thing and gladly signed the house over to his brother.

Not three weeks later, as he and Mary drove by the house on their way to run errands, he noticed a strange car out front. Later, on another pass by, a young family was playing in the yard. But it wasn't his brother's family. It wasn't anyone he knew.

Sam would later find out that his brother already had a buyer in mind for the house and had sold it to him for an enormous profit. Sam was crushed and had stopped talking to him immediately. That act suddenly made him more aware of the capacity for deception in other people. Instantly, everyone was out to get him. Day after day, the anger grew in him, until it found a permanent home in his heart. Forgiveness wasn't something he had to give, but he was willing to try anything to get Mary back.

The next day, he tried his brother again. His wife answered the phone and said he wasn't home, but that he had mentioned something about heading over to Sam's house. Thirty minutes later, his brother's car pulled into the driveway.

Sam went out to meet him. The temptation was there to punch him right in the nose, but he held back. He could tell his little brother wanted to say something and he didn't think anything he was willing to say at that moment would come out right.

His brother's head hung low as he spoke.

"Sam, I messed up. I cheated you all those years ago because I thought I had to. I was in debt up to my eyeballs and my marriage was falling apart. I didn't know of any other way to get that money. I was too proud to tell you, so I just let you hate me. Here, this is yours."

He handed Sam an envelope filled with fifty-dollar bills.

"It isn't the whole amount," he continued. "But I'm going to start making you payments. Half of what I made on the house, plus interest."

Sam stuffed the envelope back in his brother's hand and surprised himself as he pulled his sibling in for a quick but fierce hug.

"I don't want your money, just the apology. You could have told me, you know. I would have helped you out as much as I could."

His little brother looked pale. "I was so stupid. I just didn't want you to know how much I had screwed up. I would rather you think I was a slime ball than a dummy."

They both chuckled at that. The men walked inside and sat at the kitchen table.

As they talked, Sam's brother looked up at him.

"I hate to say this, but your house stinks. Where's Mary?"

Again, they laughed and soon, images appeared with not only Mary, but also Sam's extended family filling the table. A Sunday dinner done right.

Avia turned to Juliet. "Six months later, Sam came to join us here. But his heart had found peace; he lived his remaining days on earth without regret."

Juliet wiped the tears from her eyes. Was it actually possible to be happy about your own death?

Avia smiled. "And now, would you like to see the blessing that I think will bring you the most joy?"

Juliet nodded, unsure if anything could top what she had already seen but excited about what would come next.

Avia motioned to the viewing screen.

"Take a look," she said and smiled.

15 / ELLIE AT THIRTY-FIVE

Ben smoothed the dark hair that was ruffled across Ellie's forehead. It had become matted with sweat during the labor, but he thought she had never looked more beautiful.

She held their newborn baby in her arms and could not take her eyes off of him. His hair was the same raven mane as his mother's, his eyes the same radiant blue as his father's.

Visitors had been in and out that morning. Ellie's father had come by, and Ben was so relieved to see the easy manner that had fallen into place between the man and his youngest daughter. The bitterness and the distance had all faded away as they had the opportunity to experience a renewed relationship. It had all started with the grandchildren and the innocence, joy, and peace they finally brought to Ellie.

Ben had experienced a special joy himself when his daughters met their new little brother. The two girls had approached the latest addition to their family slowly, hesitating at the door when they first arrived. Neither knew or could remember what it was like to be so close to such a little person. Ben could tell that they both wanted to do everything exactly right. Even at the young ages of five and three, they were very aware of the world around them, and especially other people. Ben wondered if that was because they were adopted, though neither was fully aware of what that meant.

They had broached the subject with Isabelle softly, wanting her to know that she was a gift to them, and they were thankful for her every day. Not only had she been a cherished gift, but she was also a blessed surprise. She had come to them right at their darkest hour, when Ellie had all but given up hope.

Isabelle had been deposited one evening by a young girl from the high school down the street from the fire hall where Ben still occasionally worked as a volunteer. One of his friends had called him as soon as they received the infant, and after some time in the hospital and the miracle of the system working in their favor, Isabelle had been theirs.

Adjusting to a new baby had been hard on all of them, but Ellie had flourished during the process. Not soon after, she asked Ben if he wanted a second. For some reason, they still hadn't been able to conceive a child on their own. They began the adoption process immediately, this time in a more conventional manner, and two years later, Rebecca had joined their family.

A couple of years after that, they wanted to try adopting once again, but right before the paperwork began, Ellie began to get violently sick every morning. Even during the night, she would awaken and have to dash to the bathroom. After two weeks, she went to the doctor. And after the visit, she called Ben excitedly. Never before had she been so happy to be so ill.

The pregnancy was a difficult one, but somehow Ellie managed to cherish even that. She knew that inside her, a little life was growing again, and no matter what it took or how hard it was, she was going to do everything in her power to keep him safe.

They made it through the eighth month without incident. Two days before David's due date, Ellie's water had broken all over their living room floor, and they had rushed to the hospital.

Now, it was just the three of them alone in the hospital room, and this peaceful calm that enveloped them as David nursed and slept was almost intoxicating. There was definitely never a quiet time at home with their two young ones and now, with a third added to the mix, Ben knew he might never get another chance to say what needed to be said.

"I've waited a long time to tell you this story," he began softly, almost in a whisper. "I didn't think you would want to listen to it until you were truly happy."

Ellie smiled at him, not really listening now, though she was in fact deliriously happy. She was too enraptured with the little one in her arms to pay much attention to her husband's quiet tones.

He continued. "After we received Isabelle, I knew we were close. Then, we were given Rebecca, and I thought about telling you. But now that I see you with David, I know that you have truly reached your contentment. And after being through so much pain, you, more than anyone, deserve to be happy and to have all of your dreams come true."

She looked up at him now, and he realized he had captured her attention.

"I have been happy for a long time," she said quietly, her strength not quite back after the long ordeal from this morning. She had been in labor for eleven long hours with David. Eleven hours that at one time seemed like eternity and now felt like the blink of an eye. She would do it all over again in a second to make it to this point. A point she never quite thought she would get to. But she had been happy long before this. "When we first received Isabelle from your firehouse, I started to believe that miracles do happen. When you helped me go back to school and get my master's degree so I could become a school counselor, I finally felt fulfillment. And really, from the moment I locked onto those baby blues of yours, I knew that the right to happiness was there. You just helped me find it and accept it. And the more that we were together, the more I realized that it was okay to be happy and that nothing bad would happen because I was."

He looked at her, relieved that his wife was finally experiencing the peace and the joy that she had earned. He had asked many times in their marriage if she was happy, and though she always said she was, he had never been completely sure. Now, he was.

"Tell me your story, you silly man," she said, and he was brought back to the point at hand.

"Just listen," he cautioned as he began. "I know some of this may seem crazy, but it's all true."

Ellie was definitely listening now.

"Quite a few years ago, one of my earliest memories was of attending a funeral with my mom and dad. Vaguely, I can recall them arguing and fighting for many weeks before that. Every day when I'd come home from school, my mom would be crying. She tried to cover it up when I saw her, but I knew that something was wrong. My dad wasn't around too much, but when he was, they were always fighting. One day, I came home and my suitcase was packed. My mom's suitcase was sitting beside it by the door. She told me we were going to visit my grandma in Florida but we'd never packed the big cases before. I remember being so scared; I thought we were running away. That night, before we left, she got a call from the hospital where she worked as a nurse. One of her friends had died, and they wanted to see if she would attend the funeral with a group from the hospital. Apparently, this friend was a very close one and she felt compelled to go. She stuffed our suitcases in the closet upstairs and made me promise not to tell Daddy about the trip. She said it was going to be a surprise."

He paused and looked at Ellie. He could already see her brain churning, trying to figure out where he was going with his tale.

"Two days later, we all went to the funeral. I was surprised that my dad went, and I could tell my mom was too. I don't remember him talking to us for days before that. And every time he did, it was to yell. I remember my mom screaming about him working too many hours and ignoring his family. She said she was tired of him putting his family last, always giving us a lower priority than his job."

Ellie touched his arm softly. She knew Ben had such a close relationship with his family now, and it was hard to imagine there had ever been so much discord among them.

"I knew my mom was going to leave him, and I think he knew it too. Maybe that was why he went to the funeral that day, to show her that he didn't want to let her go. I know I definitely didn't want to move all the way to Florida and lose all of my friends.

"During the funeral, the minister spoke a lot about the nurse who had died. He praised her career as one of servitude and applauded her life spent giving to others. He talked about her family and the children she was leaving behind. And then, he said the words that I think changed my life.

"He spoke directly to the husband of the nurse who had died. He told him that the road ahead of him would be a hard one. Being a father was hard enough on its own, but for at least a little bit, he was going to have to be the father and the mother. A single parent was one of the toughest jobs out there, and he was going to need the whole community to make it through. Then, he asked all of the fathers to stand. And he prayed for them. He prayed that they would all use this opportunity to stop and examine their role in their own family. He told them that no matter what job title they had, no matter what they accomplished in life, the most important assignment they would ever complete was that of husband and father. If they didn't step up to that responsibility, there was no failure they would regret more. Nothing could be more noble or crucial than success at home."

Ellie agreed with that. Ben had been an amazing father to their children and knew he would be an especially excellent example to their son.

Ben went on. "For some reason, my dad took those words to heart. I'd never seen him cry before that day, and I've never seen him cry since then. But at that funeral, there were tears streaking down his cheeks. He took my mom's hand right then and didn't let go until we got to the car. Once they got me inside, I saw him get down on his knees in front of her and beg for her forgiveness. She cried too, and I could see how much she wanted to give him that mercy. But she had been hurt for too long and she was scared that he would go back to his old ways. I know that wasn't the first time he'd apologized."

Ellie was a little puzzled. She knew that his parents ended up together, so she wasn't quite sure where the story was headed.

"We went to Florida for a month. We were both miserable. My dad called every single day and begged my mom to come home. Finally, none of us could take it anymore. My grandma finally persuaded my mom to go back to my dad and give him one last chance. She said we could always come back if we needed to. But luckily, we didn't. When we returned home, nothing was ever the same. My parents still argued but it was nothing that lasted more than a few minutes. My dad was always at my baseball games and made it home every night for dinner. He decided he wanted to change, and he did. But I don't think any of that would have happened if we hadn't gone to the funeral."

He looked at Ellie, touching her arm as she nursed a peacefully sleeping David.

"So you see then? We were at your mom's funeral. And because of that day, my parents stayed together. I didn't move to Florida. I went to our local college. And I met you."

She tried to smile at him but couldn't manage it. She was overwhelmed with the irony, with thankfulness, and with missing her mom. But she couldn't deny that Ben's presence in her life had been her turning point.

"And you are the one who saved me," she finally whispered.

"Saved you from what?" he asked.

"From myself," she said so quietly that he almost couldn't hear. "If I hadn't had you, if I had continued down the path I was on, who knows how I would have ended up?"

Ben touched her hand then, softly but with an urgency for her to understand. "Hopefully I just helped you realize that no matter how dark it seems, there is always hope. And even when we can't see it, everything is still going according to plan."

ABOUT THE AUTHOR

Alana McIntyre penned her first short story at the tender age of seven, and her love affair with writing has continued ever since. On a daily basis she acts as head ringmaster for her three rambunctious redheads and husband while at the same time balancing her photographic and literary interests. Graduation Day is the first novel in a spiritual awakening series that chronicles the inner turmoil we all face in this world and the next. Alana is a huge fan of the iPad, the Texas Rangers, cupcakes of every flavor, and drinking hot chocolate even in the 100-degree Texas heat.

For more information, please view her website:
www.1000-pages.com

www.ingramcontent.com/pod-product-compliance
Lightning Source LLC
Chambersburg PA
CBHW031356040426
42444CB00005B/309